YouTube
WORLD
RECORDS

DON'T TRY THIS AT HOME

Some of this book's clips feature stunts performed either
by professionals or under the supervision of professionals.
Accordingly, the publishers must insist that no one attempts
to re-create or reenact any stunt or activity performed on
the featured videos.

Portable Press
An imprint of Printers Row Publishing Group
10350 Barnes Canyon Road, Suite 100, San Diego, CA 92121
www.portablepress.com • e-mail: mail@portablepress.com

Printers Row Publishing Group is a division of Readerlink Distribution
Services, LLC. Portable Press is a registered trademark of Readerlink
Distribution Services, LLC.

All notations of errors or omissions should be addressed to Portable Press,
Editorial Department, at the above address. All other correspondence
(author inquiries, permissions) concerning the content of this book should
be addressed to www.carltonbooks.co.uk.

For Portable Press:
Publisher: Peter Norton
Associate Publisher: Ana Parker
Publishing/Editorial Team: Vicki Jaeger, Tanya Fijalkowski, Lauren Taniguchi
Editorial Team: JoAnn Padgett, Melinda Allman, Dan Mansfield

For Carlton Books:
Project Editor: Chris Mitchell
Design: Katie Baxendale
Production: Lisa Hedicker
Picture Research: Steve Behan

ISBN: 978-1-68412-366-7

Printed in China

21 20 19 18 17   1 2 3 4 5

YouTube

WORLD RECORDS

ADRIAN BESLEY

PORTABLE
PRESS

San Diego, California

CONTENTS

INTRODUCTION

Welcome to the only records book that enables you to see the records being broken for yourself. Enter the short URL or scan the QR code into your phone, tablet, laptop, or computer and witness history being made across the world.

The fastest, biggest, highest, thinnest—all over the world people are united by a fascination with human achievements. We all love a record breaker. Whether it is a hundredth of a second being shaved off a famous sporting record or the first recording of a fantastically bizarre new category, we share a fascination with discovering who and what. Until now, the only thing missing has been our chance to actually see the record breakers in action.

That's where YouTube comes in. This global resource is open to anyone to upload their videos. It contains literally thousands of record-breaking clips, from the most well-known to the completely obscure. Some have millions of views, while others remain virtually undiscovered.

Among the gems available to view are Usain Bolt's amazing 100-meter sprint; the world's tallest man sharing a coffee with the world's shortest man; Nik Wallenda's nail-biting tightrope (the highest ever while blindfolded); the man who moves bucketfuls of maggots with his mouth; a woman with the world's strongest hair; and the land speed record for a toilet!

This book is your guide to the best of the record-breaking videos on YouTube. It leads you to the most exciting, the most thrilling, the most interesting, and the most ridiculous videos on the site. Just read through the brief description and then use the short URL address or the QR code to access the clip—all, of course, completely for free.

HIGH-FLYING RECORDS

Don't look down! It's time to meet some of the sky-high heroes of the record-breaking world. These are some vertigo-immune daredevils who don't know the meaning of fear.

Wingsuit Wonder

http://y2u.be/N6Zk9GO0ql0

Jhonathan Florez leaped out of a plane above Colombia in April 2012 and broke four world records in one death-defying jump. Diving from 37,265 feet, he made the highest-ever wingsuit jump, and his time of 9 minutes 6 seconds smashed the record for the longest-duration wingsuit jump. He also took the record for greatest horizontal distance flown in a wingsuit—a mammoth 16.315 miles—and flew the greatest distance ever in a wingsuit of 17.52 miles.

MULTIPLE RECORD BREAKER IN ONE FLIGHT

RECORD-BREAKING SHALLOW WATER DIVE

◀ The Greatest Flop

http://y2u.be/cur0YILfQB8

He's the King of the Belly Flops, the Prince of Paddling Pool Plunges, he's Professor Splash. The Professor (real name: Darren Taylor) is believed to be the only diver to have mastered the art of shallow water diving. Here, he is breaking his own world record at the University of Science and Technology in Trondheim, Norway, by diving 36 feet into a kiddie pool containing just 12 inches of water.

Cookie-Dunking Bungee Jump

http://y2u.be/UBf7WC19lpw

The lengths the British will go to for the love of tea and cookies, eh? In 2016, Simon Berry from Yorkshire, England, took a 240-foot bungee dive to dunk his cookie into his cup of tea. Clasping both wrists together like a diver to achieve the necessary precision, Simon's jump was perfectly judged to allow for his extended hand to dip his chocolate-coated cookie halfway into his freshly brewed cup of tea. And, to complete a perfect plunge, the cookie was still intact and nicely half melted when he returned to the platform. It was the highest bungee dunk ever.

▶

Over the Edge

http://y2u.be/-9ox62y4zsE

Imagine taking a leap from, say, the top of the Leaning Tower of Pisa, past jagged rocks, and into a small pool beneath. In August 2015, in a world-record cliff-jump attempt, Brazilian-born daredevil Laso Schaller plunged almost 200 feet from a ledge into Switzerland's famed Cascata del Salto waterfall. Six oxygen tents were aerating the water in order to give him a softer landing, but Schaller hit the water outside of his intended landing zone—at a speed of around 76 miles per hour. This high-quality video shows the death-defying jump from every angle, including the view from a camera mounted to his helmet.

HIGHS AND LOWS

These record breakers have gone to extreme heights (or as low as they can go) in order to get their names in the record books.

▼ Skate Limbo

http://y2u.be/7HEPRZuRWvc

Like many young kids, Gagan Satish, a Bangalore schoolboy, loves to get out on his roller skates. Not many, however, have a talent like Gagan's. He skated nearly 230 feet with his face just 5 inches from the ground—passing under 39 cars on the way! Gagan has been roller skating for only three years, but, even more incredibly, he is only six years old. Obviously, his experience helped him break the record; the previous holder was only five!

Breathtaking!

http://y2u.be/YtryV9qltsg

Next time you're at your local swimming pool, see how long you can hold your breath underwater. Can you do 30 seconds? Or maybe 45 seconds, if you really fill your lungs. This exercise will give you some appreciation of Canadian William Winram's 2013 record dive into the Dead Sea at Sharm el-Sheikh in Egypt. Will took a single breath and held it for 3 minutes 8 seconds, using a sled to help him descend 475 feet—as a comparison, New York's Statue of Liberty is just 300 feet tall—and a rope and monofin to speed his return to the surface.

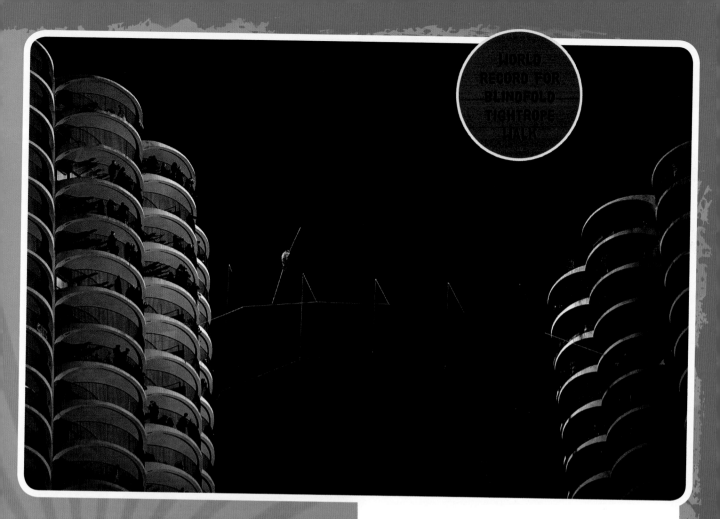

WORLD RECORD FOR BLINDFOLD TIGHTROPE WALK

▲ Windy City Wire Walk

http://y2u.be/XvzcLs3H5Jk

Despite his great-grandfather Karl falling to his death from a wire in 1978, Nik Wallenda, a seventh-generation tightrope artist, took on the record for the highest blindfolded tightrope walk. Facing winds of 24 miles per hour and with no safety net or harness, he steps along a wire suspended between Chicago's two Marina City towers. No wonder live TV broadcast the monumental walk with a 10-second delay. Even knowing he makes it, you'll watch it with your heart in your mouth.

Long Engagement

When sports stars at the top of their respective games get married, the world rejoices. But when the world's tallest basketball player, Sun Mingming, and the world's tallest handball player, Xu Yan, married in Beijing, China, on August 4, 2013, the planet went crazy in love! Standing at 7 feet 9 inches and 6 feet 1.7 inches tall, respectively, this sports power-couple stand head and shoulders above their opponents, both figuratively and literally.

WORLD'S TALLEST MARRIED COUPLE

YOUTUBE HITS RECORDS

In ten years, YouTube has grown to be a part of the daily lives of millions of people. It should be no surprise, then, that it now has its own illustrious record holders.

▶ The Song That Broke YouTube

http://youtu.be/9bZkp7q19f0

References to celebrities "breaking the Internet" are common these days, but Psy's ubiquitous hit "Gangnam Style" really did break YouTube. The South Korean singer's catchy ditty continues to break YouTube viewing records (a billion more than the next most-watched, Justin Bieber's "Baby"). In December 2014, Psy's horsey dance hit swept past 2,147,483,647 views, the maximum YouTube could count. Fortunately, the YouTube engineer had seen it coming and updated their counter to a maximum of 9.22 quintillion. How long until "Gangnam Style" reaches that?

YOUTUBE'S MOST-WATCHED VIDEO

◀ What a Tease!

http://y2u.be/iXfEc4wG208

Not so long ago, trailers for forthcoming movies were a treat to be enjoyed exclusively at the movie theater, but that was before YouTube emerged as the natural platform for building excitement around a soon-to-be-released movie. When the trailer for *Star Wars: The Force Awakens* hit YouTube in 2014, more than 112 million people watched it within a day. A year later, however, the temptation to see Emma Watson and Dan Stevens star as *Beauty and the Beast* proved too great and its trailer smashed the record with 127.6 million hits in the first 24 hours it was online.

Russian Mystery

http://y2u.be/KYniUCGPGLs

Music videos still dominate YouTube's most-watched charts, but one nonmusic title stands alone in the Top 10. An episode of the Russian cartoon "Masha i Medved" ("Masha and the Bear") has garnered an astonishing 1.8 billion views—more than Adele's "Hello" or Taylor Swift's "Shake It Off." The cartoon, which features a young girl and a friendly bear, is aimed at very young children and is incredibly popular in both Russian and its English translation. However, exactly why the "Recipe for Disaster" episode in which Masha cooks too much porridge is so popular remains a mystery to YouTube experts. Perhaps you can explain . . .

Charlie Still Bites

http://y2u.be/_OBIgSz8sSM

These days, YouTube charts are dominated by music videos and children's TV shows, but one great exception refuses to die. In May 2007, a 56-second video of a young boy and his baby brother sitting by side was posted on YouTube. *Charlie Bit My Finger Again!* became a YouTube phenomenon. It was so impish, and full of infectious laughter, and for years competed with Miley, Justin, and Taylor at the top of the viewing charts. Even now—with around 850 million views—it continues to be the most-watched "home video" on the site—the greatest viral video of them all.

▲ Adele's Big Hello

https://www.youtube.com/watch?v=YQHsXMglC9A

After a four-year absence from the recording world, London-born singing phenomenon Adele Adkins released "Hello," a moving ballad of love's labor's lost that also became the fastest song to reach one billion views on YouTube after its October 23, 2015, release. It took just 87 days to hit the top spot, breaking the 158-day record held by South Korean singer and rapper Psy's "Gangnam Style" in 2012.

FASTEST SONG TO REACH ONE BILLION VIEWS

SPEED AND ACCURACY

Another selection of quick-on-the-draw records. Here, accuracy is as important as speed. One false move could mean death, a weird haircut, or a customer questioning their receipt.

▶ A Throwaway Record

http://y2u.be/JriUEsRk8Ns

The Great Throwdini is undoubtedly the world's greatest knife thrower. Despite taking up knife throwing only at the age of 50, the Reverend Doctor David R. Adamovich (his real name) has set or broken 40 world records in throwing and catching knives and bullets. He has thrown ten 14-inch knives around a human target in just 4.29 seconds and 102 knives in one minute, and he even flings the blades while wearing a blindfold!

▶ Join the Club

http://y2u.be/6MGllE2UlII

Yeah, juggling—I know. It's definitely the most boring of circus skills, but put your prejudice aside and watch this guy in action because it's pretty amazing. In September 2016, before busy train commuters at Toronto's Union Station, Cirque du Soleil's Rudolf Janecek became the fastest five-club juggler in the world. In a whirl of silver clubs and lightning hands, Rudolph shuffles along as he completes 429 rotations during 30 seconds. In fact, Rudolf threw and caught the clubs so fast that the adjudicators had to review the video in slow-motion before awarding him the record.

FASTEST
CLUB
JUGGLER

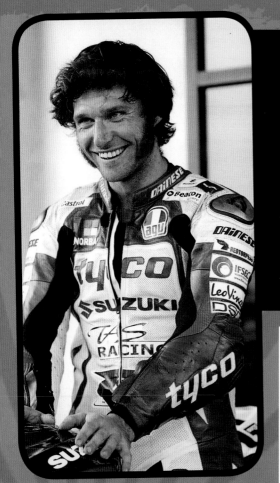

◀ Speed Freak

http://y2u.be/dvnmrHS3d9s

British motorcyclist and TV presenter Guy Martin has a passion for speed and danger. He had already held world records for the fastest speed on a gravity-power snow sled (83 miles per hour) and fastest speed in a soapbox (85 miles per hour) when, in 2016, he attempted the scarily dangerous world record for the fastest speed traveled around a Wall of Death. This old-time circus show involves riding a motorcycle horizontally around a large wooden drum-style arena. Some said it was impossible, but Guy overcame dizziness and the punishing effect of G-force on the human body to reach a staggering speed of more than 78 miles per hour.

▼ Shear Brilliance

http://y2u.be/TbUDbH6tjGs

THE FASTEST SHEEP SHEARER IN THE WORLD

Spare a thought for the poor sheep in this clip. One moment she's nice and warm in a big woolly coat, then . . . wham! Less than 15 seconds later, she's stripped down to the skin. She had no chance against New Zealand's living legend, David Fagan—who has been called "the Pelé of sheep shearing." Eleven times a world record holder, he can shear a sheep faster than most men can shave.

A Brush with Fame

http://y2u.be/eXPJo1f60j0

Like most children, Dipanshu Mishra was probably told to clean his teeth at least twice a day. Now I'm sure Dipanshu always polishes up his pearly whites diligently, but he's also been practicing with the brush to earn his place among the record breakers. His is a strange record, but one that is oddly compelling to watch: Dipanshu balances a spinning basketball on the end of his toothbrush—and he keeps it spinning for an astonishing 42.92 seconds. That's certainly a feat, especially considering he doesn't even play basketball!

THE NEED FOR SPEED!

Whoosh! There's no substitute for pure lightning-strike speed, and these guys have all taken the needle into the red with power, guts, and a little madness.

▶ Lightning Bolt

http://y2u.be/4gUW1JikaxQ

"I am trying to be one of the greatest, to be among Ali and Pelé," said Usain Bolt, prior to competing in his final Olympics. That he was going to succeed was never in doubt. Usain Bolt is the fastest human being ever timed, with a list of world records as long as his magnificent, striding legs. At the Rio 2016 games, Bolt won gold in the 100 meters, the 200 meters, and the 4x100-meter relay. That meant he'd earned three gold medals at three consecutive Olympics and completed a "triple-triple." Truly a living legend.

THE FASTEST 100-METER SPRINT ON RECORD

▶ Smash!

http://y2u.be/7HTeG0CmKbU

For all the power of the tennis serve and the intensity of the squash shot, badminton is the real seat of power among racket sports. Tennis serves reach 160 miles per hour, squash pushes the limit to 170 miles per hour, but badminton smashes regularly break the 200 mile-per-hour barrier. Chinese player Fu Hai Feng (with his partner Cai Yun) is the world men's badminton doubles champion and king of the smash. His 2005 record of 206 miles per hour has been beaten in racket promotional videos but never in real competition.

▼ Two-Wheel Triumph

http://y2u.be/PP-7WX12H2I

They call him the Red Baron, but the only things Éric shoots down are world records. Daredevil Éric possesses the land-speed cycling record on both snow and gravel. He hit a speed of 107 miles per hour on the gravel slopes of the Cerro Negro volcano in Nicaragua moments before crashing and breaking several ribs. He then opted for the softer landing of snow and recorded a speed of 138 miles per hour in Les Arcs ski resort in the French Alps.

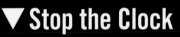

THE FASTEST BIKE ON SNOW AND GRAVEL

▼ Stop the Clock

https://www.youtube.com/watch?v=xG91krXuxyw

"Oh my God! From lane eight, a world record . . . I have never seen anything from 200 to 400 like that," shouted Michael Johnson as he watched his 400-meter world record change hands in Rio 2016. "That was a massacre from Wayde van Niekerk. He just put those guys away." This was the standout athletic performance of the games, as the South African not only shaved 0.15 seconds off a record that had stood since 1999, but also became the first man to win an Olympic 400-meter title from lane 8.

Handstand Finish

http://y2u.be/9p8LZVZoUzk

Tameru Zegeye is known as "The Miracle Man of Ethiopia." Born with deformed feet and unable to use his legs, Tameru learned to walk on his hands. His agility earned him a place in a circus, but he has proved his athletic skills as well. While visiting the small town of Fürth in north Bavaria, Germany, the 32-year-old completed a 100-meter sprint on crutches in a world record time of 56 seconds. What is really amazing is Tameru's technique, an incredible gravity-defying combination of balance, strength, and coordination.

EXTREME WEATHER

Witness the shock and devastation brought by these record-breaking natural disasters—hurricanes, tsunamis, and other calamitous events—in tense and dramatic footage uploaded to YouTube.

▶ Weather Report

http://y2u.be/unV5KcSrY-I

This clip went viral and became known as the *Hurricane Charley Gas Station* video. It shows a gas station in Charlotte Harbor, Florida, being torn apart by winds of more than 155 miles per hour. Hurricane Charley, classed as Category 4 (the second strongest band), was the strongest hurricane to hit southwest Florida for 50 years. These winds were the strongest ever caught on video and were captured by Mike Theiss, whose wonderful weather films appear on the Ultimate Chase channel.

The Super Tsunami

http://y2u.be/yN6EgMMrhdI

On July 9, 1958, an earthquake caused a landslide at the head of Lituya Bay in Alaska. It generated a mega-tsunami measuring between 100 feet and 300 feet, the highest tsunami wave in recorded history. This fascinating four-minute BBC clip tells the story of the tsunami, illuminated by the incredible tale of two witnesses, the only survivors from the boats out that day. It has been viewed more than 5 million times.

▶ Hailstone from Hell

http://y2u.be/w47HxYgG7bg

The hailstones that fell in Vivian, South Dakota, in 2010 weren't unpleasant, they were downright dangerous. As huge ice balls pummeled the ground and houses, locals described it as like having someone throw bricks from an airplane. After the storm, Les Scott picked the largest hailstone to put in his daiquiri, but then thought better of it. He contacted the National Weather Service, who revealed that both its weight of 1.9375 pounds (31 ounces) and its circumference of 18.5 inches made this particular hailstone a record breaker.

▲ Mount Devastation

http://y2u.be/lhU6jml6NY4

Mount St. Helens is a volcano in Washington State. In 1980, an earthquake caused the north face to slide away, creating the largest landslide ever recorded. The landslide triggered explosions that sent rocks, ash, volcanic gas, and steam into the air at more than 300 miles per hour and created a column of ash that reached over 15 miles into the atmosphere in only 15 minutes. This video, created from a series of photographs, reveals the enormity of this colossal act of nature.

AMAZING ANIMAL RECORDS

The animal kingdom has its champions, too. A safari through YouTube's wildlife clips reveals some fascinating and surprising records and some incredible footage from the wild world.

▶ Monkey Business

http://y2u.be/zsXP8qeFF6A

About 98 percent of their genome is identical to humans, so it is not surprising that chimpanzees are regarded as the smartest of animal species. They can make and use tools, hunt in organized groups, and have shown they are capable of empathy, altruism, and self-awareness. Over and above all this, they are adept at computer skills—and in the case of Ayumu, featured in this video, can beat a human at memory games.

CHIMP WITH A MEMORY SUPERIOR TO HUMANS

◀ Big Bug

http://y2u.be/tBaRwtzFBbo

The Maoris call it "the God of Ugly Things." A little rude? Looking at a picture of the giant weta, you might think it's a little like a cricket and not really that unsightly, but see the insect in real life and—whoa—it's the size of a rodent. Once common in New Zealand, the world's biggest insect is now believed to live on only Little Barrier Island, about 50 miles northeast of Auckland. Weighing more than a sparrow, this creature is too heavy to jump, let alone fly, but it can pack a nasty nip with its oversize pincers.

▼ Don't Have a Cow

https://www.youtube.com/watch?v=JMWrXkLGCwA

The world's tallest cow ever officially recorded was Blossom, a female Holstein. She came in at a whopping height of 74.8 inches—that's more than 6 feet tall! Blossom was first recognized by the Guinness World Records in Orangeville, Illinois, in May 2014, but went on to receive another honor, World's Tallest Cow Ever, in 2015.

▲ Dive Bomb

http://y2u.be/r7lglchYNew

Most people can name the cheetah as the fastest mammal on earth, but the fastest creature on the planet? The answer is the peregrine falcon. Its horizontal cruising speeds reach up to only 50–65 miles per hour; but when in a hunting dive, known as a stoop, this bird of prey regularly flies more than 150 miles per hour—more than twice the speed of the cheetah—and has been recorded at 242 miles per hour. They plunge at such a rate that they kill their prey with a single blow.

WORLD'S TALLEST COW

No Slouch

http://y2u.be/rR4L6Gil1AE

"When Bertie gets going, there's no stopping him," the owner of Adventure Valley, a children's park in County Durham in England, told the *Guardian* newspaper, clearly suspecting that Bertie was the Usain Bolt of the tortoise world. Indeed, when Bertie was put to the test in September 2015, he smashed the record, covering 18 feet in 19.59 seconds. This was twice as fast as the previous time of 43.7 seconds, which had stood since 1977. Bertie's speed equates to sprinting a mighty 0.6 miles per hour, so all hail the fastest tortoise in the world.

FREAKY FOOD RECORDS

The world of food and drink showcases some marvelous records, including enormous vegetables, oversize fast food, and a time-honored crazy method of cracking open champagne bottles.

▶ Burger King

http://y2u.be/KQ0uDYdpHfs

Two all-beef patties, special sauce, lettuce, cheese, pickles, onions—on a sesame seed bun. It's what we all know as a McDonald's Big Mac. And Matt Stonie is going to eat 25 of these? In less than an hour? We're talking around 11 pounds of fast food, packing a hefty 13,250 calories. Popular YouTuber Matt, however, is nothing if not dedicated to his cause and, after getting over the $120 damage to his credit card at the drive-thru, he settles gamely to the task. Have a look. It's an entertaining watch, but perhaps not best viewed on a full stomach.

Grim Reaper

http://y2u.be/3zhym9oUSGU

The "Carolina Reaper," a crossbreed between a Ghost chili pepper and a Red Habanero pepper, has been rated as the world's hottest chili pepper. It averages 1,569,300 on the Scoville heat scale, making it more than 900 times hotter than Tabasco sauce. There are enough chili pepper-eating videos on YouTube to show what excruciating results can occur, but despite that, the Danish TV host, Bubber, is foolish enough to step up to the plate.

Super Saber

http://y2u.be/k_vfg1dJito

Napoleon is reputed to have declared: "Champagne! In victory one deserves it; in defeat one needs it." It was his troops who first popularized "sabering" champagne bottles—severing the neck from the bottle with the flat edge of a saber. It is a precise skill—cutting through the glass at an exact stress point—and is one perfected by Mitch Ancoana as he opens a world record 34 bottles in a minute. An achievement worth celebrating.

▼ Onion King

http://y2u.be/ZClfa3L0dtY

Tony Glover was named King of the Onions when he managed to produce a mighty onion weighing 18 pounds 11 ounces. Using seed bought from the previous record holder, Peter Glazebrook, Tony says it took nearly a year to grow his mighty specimen. He gives them nitrogen-rich food and makes sure the humidity is just right. Giant onions have trebled in size since 1985 and word has it that the Holy Grail of onions—the 20 pounder—is just around the corner.

◀ Pizza the Action

http://y2u.be/IT09m7mOltM

In front of 6,000 spectators, Pali Grewal, a pizza chef in London, England, made three large pizzas in 39.1 seconds—a pizza every 13 seconds. The contestants at the competition had to hand stretch fresh dough, spread the tomato sauce, and top three large pizzas—one pepperoni, one mushroom, and one cheese. Quality was scrutinized as two judges inspected each aspect of the process. If the pizza was not perfect, it was returned to the competitor to be remade.

RECORD-BREAKING PEOPLE

Those born at the extremes of the physical spectrum—the tallest, the smallest, etc.—have always held a special fascination. These clips reveal the human beings behind some of the statistics.

▶ A Tall Story

http://y2u.be/RwzMWuAxANw

Robert Pershing Wadlow from Alton, Illinois, is the tallest recorded person ever to have lived. He was born in 1918 and, by the time he was eight years old, he was 6 feet 2 inches tall. By the time he was 19, he had reached a height of 8 feet 11.1 inches—the tallest living man is a mere 8 feet 2 inches. Unfortunately, Robert would live only a few years more after an infection in his foot spread to his body. He was known as the Gentle Giant and more than 27,000 people attended his funeral.

THE TALLEST MAN WHO EVER LIVED

Towering Teen

http://y2u.be/hBq06yJYqLQ

Teenage growth spurts are a common phenomenon. One minute your nephew is a 4-foot 12-year-old and the next time you see him he's 14 and pushing 6 feet. However, American Broc Brown is something else. Because of a genetic disorder known as Sotos syndrome or cerebral gigantism, he's been growing up to 6 inches a year throughout his teens. Broc is now 19 and stands 7 feet 8 inches tall. About to leave "teenagerdom" behind, Broc is on course to become the world's tallest man. The current record is held by Turkish farmer Sultan Kosen, who stands at 8 feet 2 inches.

◀ Animal Magnetism

http://y2u.be/rbUuzCRa3Ug

Former kickboxing coach Etibar Elchyev, from the Eurasian country of Georgia, is known as "Magnetic Man." Ever since he discovered his ability to attract metal objects to his body, Etibar has been setting new records. Here, in December 2013, we find him putting spoons on his chest and back—53 in total, a new world record. An excellent talent, but he must dread visiting the cafeteria. Scientists claim his skin is not magnetic but merely "sticky." Whatever . . . he's still in a magnetic field of his own!

THE MOST SPOONS ON A HUMAN BODY

▶ Inseparable Brothers

http://y2u.be/gPcijt2Wals

Twin brothers Ronnie and Donnie Galyon were born healthy in Dayton, Ohio, in October 1951. Joined at the waist, they each had arms, legs, and separate hearts but shared a stomach and some organs. Sixty-three years later, they were still joined and could celebrate being the oldest-ever conjoined twins, beating Italian brothers Giacomo and Giovanni Battista Tocci, who were born in 1877. The twins spent their lives from the age of four in circus sideshows but have now retired to live with their younger brother.

THE LONGEST-LIVING TWINS IN THE WORLD

WILD AND WACKY

Hidden away in the nooks and corners of YouTube are some odd and eccentric records. Here are just a few . . .

◤ Sealed with a Kiss

https://www.youtube.com/watch?v=cbedCMLO1EA

A married couple, Ekkachai and Laksana Tiranarat, locked lips for 46 hours 24 minutes in a kissathon contest in Pattaya, Thailand. They were the winners from 14 competing couples, who were all required to have a marriage certificate or a letter from both parents. However, it wasn't all for love. They were competing for a diamond ring and a cash prize! And to really ruin the romance, they were allowed to eat, drink, and use the lavatory—provided they did not break their embrace.

THE LONGEST KISS IN HISTORY

Cup Winner

http://y2u.be/RsBdA2S2E-8

Sport stacking is a game in which competitors stack plastic cups in specific sequences as quickly as possible. The toughest of the disciplines is the "cycle" in which 12 cups are stacked in three different ways, including pyramid formations. Fifteen-year-old William Orrell is the indisputable king of stacking—holding the record for all three individual disciplines. This clip shows his incredible record-breaking cycle stack at the first-ever Nation's Capital Open Sport Stacking Tournament, where he takes just 5.1 seconds to finish.

◀ Tattoo Love

http://y2u.be/QIULSyKlrGY

Couples need a shared interest and there's no prize for guessing Chuck Helmke and Charlotte Guttenberg's common passion. Chuck, at the age of 75, and Charlotte, a sprightly 65-year-old, met in a tattoo studio in 2006. Charlotte was just discovering the joys of body art, while Chuck had begun covering his body in ink five years earlier. Now, they are officially the male and female most-tattooed senior citizens world record holders. Displaying a colorful array of intricate tattoos, both boast more than 90 percent body coverage, with even their shaved heads inked. There's not a lot anyone can do to beat that!

MOST-TATTOOED SENIOR CITIZENS

▶ Dead Cool

http://y2u.be/xtHzRjnoXKw

In November 2014, 509 slightly scary-looking skeletons in ball gowns and brimmed hats gathered in the city center in Mexico City to set the world record for the largest gathering of Catrinas. The figure of Catrina, known as the Elegant Death, was created and immortalized in works by artists Guadalupe Posada and Diego Rivera and is now a traditional part of Mexico's Day of the Dead celebrations. People dress as the skeletal character to visit cemeteries and share offerings and food with the dead and their families.

A RECORD GATHERING OF CATRINAS

SPORTS RECORD BREAKERS

There's more to sports than winning. There are records to be broken. These athletes have etched their names in the history of their sports—however strange!

▶ Alley-oop!

https://www.youtube.com/watch?v=H9SF2YIKRY8

On the tiny island of Tasmania, off Australia's South Coast, a truly ridiculous world record was broken. From the top of the island's Gordon Dam—415 feet tall—three friends made the basketball shot of a lifetime. Plunging downward, seemingly forever, the ball found its way into the hoop to ecstatic cheers all around. Viewed more than eight million times on YouTube so far, the How Ridiculous Aussie boys, who travel the world looking for epic trick shots, have officially thrown the farthest basketball hoop shot ever. Wow!

Xtreme 19th

http://y2u.be/iOWR7O1oSgU

The Legend Golf 18-hole course in South Africa has a bonus hole—the "Xtreme 19th"—the highest and longest par three golf hole in the world. The tee sits on top of a cliff on Hanglip Mountain, more than 1,400 feet above a green carved in the shape of the continent of Africa—it takes nearly 30 seconds for the ball to hit the ground. Drill a hole-in-one and you win $1 million, but no one has yet bettered a two-shot birdie.

WORLD RECORD-BREAKING BASKET

◀ Skyfall

https://www.youtube.com/watch?v=2YSQ7-e-fZ0

In December 2016, teammates Laurent Koscielny, Francis Coquelin, Theo Walcott, and Nacho Monreal, of the English soccer team Arsenal, each attempted to break the record for the highest-altitude soccer ball dropped and controlled. It was England forward Theo Walcott who showed the necessary skill, not only bringing a ball dropped from a height of 111.5 feet under control first time, but also keeping it off the ground for four more touches. It's not a tactic the team has employed before, but if you see them launching the ball skyward in a game, you'll know who they expect to be underneath it.

High Heel Hotfoot

http://y2u.be/WJ2DC2X1e5k

Running in high heels can be a risky operation. You can end up with a broken heel or a sprained ankle. However, not Julia Plecher. In a 100-meter sprint, all the stiletto-clad teenager from Germany broke was a world record. She really does cut a dash, running the distance in under 15 seconds despite wearing a figure-hugging outfit that matches her gold high heels. Keep watching and you'll see Julia triumph in a stiletto race in Berlin—wearing a 3.3-inch heel!

▶ Clogged Up

http://y2u.be/2CdYF41M6rw

Australian Rugby Union hero Drew Mitchell is his country's highest World Cup try scorer. However, the Toulon winger, who has played more than 70 times for Australia, is also a serial record breaker. On the Sky Sports Rugby TV channel, he became joint holder of the records for both the most rugby passes and the most drop goals in a minute. He then set the record for the most apples crushed with the bicep in one minute (it was 14) and went on to perform this intriguing feat: the fastest 100 meters in clogs. Wearing the heavy wooden, Klomp-style clog common to the Netherlands, Drew hit the finish line in just 14.43 seconds.

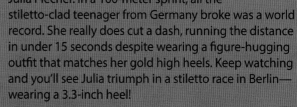

FASTEST 100 METERS WEARING CLOGS

THEME PARK RECORDS

Scream if you want to go faster! Actually, it isn't possible to go any faster than on some of these record-breaking rides—but you may find yourself screaming anyway.

▼ Viennese Whirl

http://y2u.be/UATJDA35wXk

All this speed and spinning getting too much for you? Come with us to Vienna, the capital of Austria, famous for Mozart, cake . . . and a chairoplane 384 feet high! The Prater Turm (tower) is as high as a 33-story building, from which fun seekers "fly" at a speed of 37 miles per hour. The world's highest flying-swing ride floats its guests on a seat that would easily clear the Statue of Liberty's torch and Big Ben's clock-tower spire and gives them a spinning vista of the city.

FASTEST, LONGEST, TALLEST DIVE COASTER

THE WORLD'S TALLEST SWING RIDE

Scream Machine

http://y2u.be/paGAtMORJag

Cedar Point in Sandusky, Ohio, seems determined to retain its reputation as the "roller coaster capital of the world." Its 2016 summer addition, Valravn, is the tallest (223 feet), fastest (75 mph), and longest (3,415 feet) dive coaster in the world. As this terrifying front-seat view shows, it climbs to give riders a superb view of Lake Erie before the fun begins. They are sent on a 200-foot, 90-degree free fall, before a loop-the-loop section that turns them upside-down three times. Hands up, who's ready to go round again?

▼ Vomit Comet

http://y2u.be/qqN9PDS3hOc

People have been known to line up for more than 4 hours to ride for just 2 minutes 45 seconds on the Smiler at Alton Towers, a theme park in England. It is the roller coaster with the most inversions (turning riders upside down and back again) in the world. There are 14 different inversions of seven different kinds, from the common corkscrew, cobra, and dive loops to the rarer double batwing and sea-serpent twists. Confused? Never mind, climb aboard and hold tight!

Fast Formula

http://y2u.be/ijuQwnfBBZw

The Formula Rossa roller coaster in Abu Dhabi's Ferrari World boasts acceleration from 0 to 60 miles per hour in just 2 seconds and reaches a world record 149 miles per hour. In 2010, Felipe Massa and Fernando Alonso, Formula One motor-racing drivers, took their seats in the fastest roller coaster on the planet. Although their bodies are used to being flung around at ridiculously high speeds, their faces are usually encased in helmets. Just watch as the G-force hits these seasoned speed merchants.

RECORD-BREAKING TWISTS ON A ROLLER COASTER

SCARY AND SHOCKING!

Delve into the lucky dip of the world of records and who knows what'll emerge. You could find some hair-raising danger, interesting collections, and, sometimes, something truly, truly bizarre.

DEATH ROAD
WORLD'S MOST
DANGEROUS

▲ Rocky Road

http://y2u.be/zGA3qXQs1wE

The North Yungas Road in Bolivia is 43 miles long and 2,000 feet high, and it claims around 300 lives a year. No wonder it is called the Death Road. Perils along the Most Dangerous Road in the World include rock avalanches, fog, and trucks squeezing past each other on its loose-stone surface. Often a single track only 10 feet wide, it has no guard rails—just sheer drops down the cliff edges. The route does, however, offer some stunning scenery.

▼ Selfie-Made Man

http://y2u.be/CIGajvF89NQ

In February 2016, at the *Zoolander 2* premiere in London, England, Hollywood star Ben Stiller set a world record for the longest selfie-stick picture. His snap featured members of the cast, including costars Penelope Cruz and Clive Owen. Less than a month later, London-based YouTuber James Ware constructed a 31-foot stick—a whole three feet longer than Ben's. As he attempted his shot, James was moved on from London's Trafalgar Square by an irate security guard and had to settle for a less-celebrated background. His selfie has no stars, just a bemused passerby, but no one ever said records have to be glamorous.

Walk the Plank

http://y2u.be/KbtZfzxX44o

How far are you prepared to go for a breathtaking view? If you would happily walk along a seemingly rickety plank attached to the side of a mountain cliff hundreds of feet high, then Mount Hua in China could be your ideal destination. The plankway doesn't lead anywhere—just to a stunning bird's-eye view of the surrounding mountains—and you have to return the same way, negotiating your way past those coming in the opposite direction. Overcome your fears, however, and you, too, can claim to have taken the world's most dangerous hiking trail.

Human Fireball

http://y2u.be/hICWU9HC7ts

Fire-protective clothing is available. It's worn by motor-racing drivers and movie stunt men. However, it's not for Anthony Britton. He put on three pairs of overalls, a few balaclavas, and a motorcycle helmet for his attempt on the world record for fire running. Hundreds of spectators assembled in a park in Croydon, England, to watch Anthony, an experienced escapologist, soak himself in gasoline, set himself on fire, and run at full speed across the grass. He completed an awesome 595 feet before calling in his team to douse the flames with fire extinguishers.

▶ Blown Away

http://y2u.be/AdtSdVop6V0

The James Bond franchise of movies has a long history of breaking a plethora of records. However, its latest achievement is arguably the most earth-shattering of them all. The climax of *Spectre*, the twenty-fourth Bond movie in the series, featured the largest movie-stunt explosion ever as Blofeld's desert base was detonated to kingdom come in front of the movie's stars, Daniel Craig and Madeleine Swann. Shot on June 29, 2015, in Erfoud, Morocco, the blast used 2,224 gallons of fuel and 73 pounds of explosives. The sequence might have lasted just 7.5 seconds, but it was one memorable blast.

DON'T TRY THIS AT HOME!

How desperate can you be to get your name in the record books? These record breakers seem to feel no pain as they take one or more of their senses to the limit.

Candles in the Wind

http://y2u.be/kvGa-OXORhw

It's not big and it's not smart—but you have to admit it is kind of cool. File this in the not-to-try-at-home folder, but do take a look at 28-year-old Filipino Ronald Cabañas extinguishing five lit candles with his own butt fan. In an extraordinary display of controlled flatulence, Ronald, using what can only be described as a homemade fart trumpet, puts out the candles in less than 30 seconds. It is a fine skill, but it's difficult to see how Ronald, a farmer and sometime porter, can make a career of it.

▶ Pin Face

http://y2u.be/pS2AszO0z44

GREATEST NUMBER OF CLOTHESPINS ON FACE

We've all got a skill lurking somewhere, it's just a matter of finding it. Kelvin Mercado, 36 years old, discovered he had a unique talent for clipping clothespins onto his face. Now he's a world record holder. Clothespins are attached in neat formation to every loose, and not so loose, piece of skin as well as to his lips and nose. Altogether he managed to clip on 163 clothespins—and it is something of a sight.

▼ Saucy Drinker

http://y2u.be/Q60mABHsSxM

The bartender in *Back to the Future Part III* refers to it as "wake-up juice," but just the sight of the familiar bottle of Tabasco sauce is enough to strike fear into the heart of many a diner. Its three simple ingredients—red chili peppers, salt, and distilled white vinegar—pack a punch measuring 2,500–5,000 SHU on the Scoville heat scale. Hats off then to Andrew Hajinikitas, who is prepared to risk his dignity by downing two bottles in 30 seconds live on television!

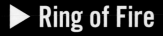

Tastes a Little Sharp?

http://y2u.be/zUeUpAhq4Gw

This is complete madness. Consuming even the smallest piece of glass can kill a person. It can wound the mouth, throat, stomach, intestines, and bowels as it passes through the digestive system. And yet, 22-year-old Potesh Talukdar from Assam, India, seems

to have no problem seeing off a whole cocktail glass full of glass accompanied only by some lemon juice. Amazingly, he does it all in just 1 minute 27 seconds. If you want to skip to the action, it starts around 6 minutes into the clip.

▶ Ring of Fire

https://www.youtube.com/watch?v=F--nCc58sTc

At South Africa's largest gathering of motorcyclists, known as the "Rhino Rally," on September 5, 2014, motorcycle enthusiasts Enrico Schoeman and André de Kock turned up the heat for their next record-breaking feat—riding a bright pink motorcycle and sidecar through a burning tunnel of fire and flames 395 feet long! Afterward, driver Enrico Schoeman admitted, "I was so disoriented by the heat, I couldn't see where I was going." Wow!

LONGEST MOTORCYCLE RUN THROUGH TUNNEL OF FIRE

THIRST-QUENCHING RECORDS

It's not just drinking the liquid stuff quickly (although, boy, can they guzzle), but shaking it, sucking it, carrying it, and even performing mass scientific experiments with it!

Lager Top

http://y2u.be/1_e9oTrrf6E

It can be difficult enough getting through the bar with three drinks in your hands, so a round of applause is surely due for Oliver Struempfel. He works at the traditional Gillemoos beer festival in the Bavarian town of Abensberg and managed to carry a record 27 one-liter steins of lager. The effort won Oliver the competition for carrying as many full mugs as possible over a distance of 130 feet. No mean feat considering the total weight exceeds 132 pounds, about the same as a small adult.

Open Wide

http://y2u.be/7C5Rc6ny2tY

Mumbai science teacher Dinesh Shivnath Upadhyay is a record obsessive. His 176 records span many categories, but there is one section that will leave you gaping in amazement. Dinesh is known as "Maximouth" due to his ability to fill his mouth with grapes, onions, pencils, golf balls, candles, and a host of other objects. His greatest achievement was surely stuffing 1,001 straws in his mouth—a task made even more difficult because the rules state that straws must have a minimum diameter of 0.25 inch and must remain in the mouth for a minimum of 10 seconds.

▶ Flip Out

http://y2u.be/INb2FChnoIQ

As 2017 began, bottle-flipping had reached epidemic proportions. Kids everywhere were flicking a partially filled plastic bottle in the hope it would land on its base. Schools were banning the practice and Mike Senatore, the man whose viral video had launched the craze, went online to apologize for distracting the nation's youth. Out in Sweden, things had gone crazier. With a 130-liter bottle supplied by supermarket chain Lidl, two YouTubers ventured to the middle of a bridge to attempt the world's biggest bottle flip...

BIGGEST BOTTLE-FLIP

▲ A Splash of Cola

http://y2u.be/uQ05eALMBEo

As every schoolchild knows, Mentos and cola make for the best science lesson ever. No one remembers the point, but if all goes well they create a terrific fountain. More than 500 Cincinnatians gathered in the city's Fountain Square in 2007 to launch the largest number of Mentos geysers to be set off at once in one location. The splash-off was synchronized, leading to an fabulous spray of cola—and a sticky mess in the middle of town.

▼ Milking It

http://y2u.be/kBFugzV1KxI

Kobayashi (also see page 107) shows his awesome power of consumption. Here, he is at Uncle Bob's Self Storage in Upper Saddle River, New Jersey, tipping a gallon of milk down his gullet in just 20 seconds. According to the clip's description, Kobayashi had set a record of eating 13 cupcakes in a minute, "so he needed to wash it down." Considering human stomachs are said to be able to contain about 3.5 quarts, it's difficult to imagine where it is all going.

Champion Guzzler

http://y2u.be/EmZGzoRXPP0

More than a million people have watched this amazing display on YouTube. The short clip features a Japanese TV show where Ken Domon from Hokkaido chugs down a 1.5-liter bottle of water in less than 5 seconds. It takes a lot of skill just to get the water out of the bottle in that time. Watch for the briefest pause as he lets the bottle expand before crushing it again, and forcing the last few gulps out.

THE BIGGEST!

When it comes to record breaking, size is definitely important. The biggest . . . is always one of the most popular of the records categories. Here are a few colossal contributors.

Get a Grip

https://www.youtube.com/watch?v=xPqv7xN1iIU

The pen is mightier than the sword, it is often said. In the case of the enormous pen made by Archarya Makunuri Srinivasa of Hyderabad, India, it certainly leaves a bigger mark after being officially recorded as the largest ballpoint pen ever constructed. Mr. Srinivasa's almighty pen measures 18.04 feet in length—38 times the size of a regular ballpoint pen—and weighs 82.08 pounds. The pen is completely functional, if not entirely practical!

THE WORLD'S BIGGEST EGG

▶ Egg-straordinary!

http://y2u.be/aNUW6DL7LXw

The largest bird egg ever seen was put up for sale at Christie's auction house in 2013 and fetched £66,675 ($101,813) at auction. The elephant bird's egg is 1 foot long and nearly 9 inches in diameter—around 100 times larger than the average chicken's egg. Extinct since the seventeenth century, elephant birds were found only on the island of Madagascar. Flightless, ostrichlike birds, they grew up to 11 feet tall.

Game On

http://y2u.be/GXA76kv5Zeo

There's no such thing as a quick game of Monopoly, especially if you're playing at Studentenvereniging Ceres, a university in Wageningen, Netherlands. In November 2016, students and staff created the world's largest board game, building a Monopoly board that measured an impressive 9,700 square feet—that's about the size of one and a half football fields! After linking 804 individual panels to form the enormous board, students attempted to roll the 3-foot-plus-high dice to begin the game. Needless to say, they passed Go and went directly into the record books.

▼ Off the Wall

http://y2u.be/EptwF6cZMWg

Of all the records set in Brazil's Olympic year, this is the most eye-catching. Artist Eduardo Kobra designed a huge mural called *Etnias*, meaning "Ethnicities," on a wall of the Olympic Boulevard in Rio de Janeiro. The colorful spray-painted mural depicts the faces of indigenous people from five different continents. Using 180 buckets of acrylic paint and 3,500 cans of spray paint, the painting stands 51 feet high and stretches for 560 feet. It's the largest spray-painted mural in the world, and it took Kobra and his team two months to complete.

THE WORLD'S BIGGEST MURAL

THE MORE, THE MERRIER!

Ah, mass participation! A chance to meet other bizarrely dressed folk, to stretch your legs in unison at a stadium, or to dance slightly out of step alongside hundreds of others.

▼ Zombie Apocalypse (almost)

http://y2u.be/QkqC6Fni2KE

They bill the Zombie Pub Crawl as the World's Greatest Undead Party with brain-eating competitions, live pop acts, a "Trapped in the Closet Sing-Along," and a zombie fun run! Minneapolis has been hosting the living dead (or people dressed up as them) annually since 2005. The original 500 zombies have multiplied until, in 2014, more than 15,000 people were officially counted stumbling around in a stupefied manner. It was the official record for a zombie gathering.

RECORD-BREAKING NuMBER OF ZOMBIES

▲ Pillow Talk

http://y2u.be/KQ_SYI9vlkc

Nobody wants to see fighting at a sports stadium, but maybe we can make an exception for CHS Field, the home of Minnesota baseball team St. Paul Saints. At the end of the second inning of the Saints' game against the Winnipeg Goldeyes, a battle broke out—among all 6,261 of the spectators. This was a mass display of that friendliest of confrontations—the pillow fight. Provided with weapons by a local pillow company, the crowd, staff, and mascots (although sadly not the players) attacked their neighbors with their nighttime bolsters. It was the biggest pillow fight in the world—ever!

▶ Wing Chun Fun!

https://www.youtube.com/watch?v=9nqMKA64iSs

Wing chun is China's most popular close-combat martial art (and the world's most popular form of kung fu) and involves striking and grappling with an opponent with force and precision for self-defense. On January 8, 2015, the stage was set for the largest wing chun display ever recorded, taking place in Sichuan Province in Chengdu, China. Exactly 10,021 wing chunners, organized by the Sichuan Southwest Vocational College of Civil Aviation, turned up kicking, punching, and "chi gerking" their way to a new world record.

LARGEST WING CHUN DISPLAY

◀ Car Cramming

http://y2u.be/cp8xJRFirAM

Fitting as many people as possible into a small car has always been a popular record. The introduction of the updated BMW Mini has given the sport a renaissance. This all-women team crammed into the car's seats, squeezed onto the dashboard, and slid into the footwells. Four more compacted themselves in the trunk—creating a new record of 28. See out the clip for the heart-stopping moment when it looks like the doors won't open to let them out.

GREATEST NUMBER OF PEOPLE IN A MINI

Ho Ho Whoa!

http://y2u.be/uoW2A_vqwpQ

Santa Claus traditionally sails through the air on his reindeer-pulled sled. Well, not in Bondi Beach in Sydney, Australia, he doesn't. In the world-famous surfing resort, Santa Claus comes ashore on a surfboard—and not just one, but hundreds of them! In December 2015, 320 surfing Santas broke the world record for the largest surf lesson. In their red suits and (some) white beards, the Santas took part in a day-long surfing masterclass in aid of a local charity. So, if your presents don't arrive this Christmas, maybe Santa's still catching a wave out in Bondi.

OPER SD

WILD WEATHER RECORDS

Mother Nature is a prodigious record breaker and produces some of the most spectacular events you can see on YouTube. Just watch the disintegrating iceberg, dramatic twister, and other gripping footage on these pages.

Tip of the Iceberg

http://y2u.be/hC3VTgIPoGU

More than 20 million people have watched this amazing clip from the documentary *Chasing Ice*. The footage shows the historic breakup at the Ilulissat Glacier in western Greenland—the largest iceberg calving ever filmed. Glacial calving happens when an iceberg breaks off from the larger ice shelf, in this case a piece measuring 1.8 cubic miles. The Ilulissat (aka Jakobshavn) Glacier produces about 10 percent of all Greenland icebergs with about 39.2 billion tons of icebergs calving off every year.

It's a Twister!

http://y2u.be/Q7X3fyId2U0

During the evening of May 31, 2013, the widest tornado in recorded history occurred over rural areas of central Oklahoma. It was 2.6 miles wide at its widest point and tracked across 16.2 miles. The storm, with accompanying wind speeds of more than 295 miles per hour, fortunately struck mostly in rural areas. Even so, eight people lost their lives as a result of the tornado. All of them were killed in vehicles—either they were trying to flee by outdriving the twister or they were storm chasers filming the cataclysmic event.

THE WIDEST TORNADO EVER RECORDED

RECORD-BREAKING LIGHTNING STORMS

▲ Everlasting Lightning

https://www.youtube.com/watch?v=edrAL2t99kE

In 2014, an area of northwestern Venezuela, where the Catatumbo River meets Lake Maracaibo, was officially recognized as having the most frequent lightning storms. Known as Relámpago del Catatumbo—the Catatumbo Lightning—this "everlasting storm" appears almost every night. Averaging 28 lightning strikes per minute for up to 10 hours at a time, it can spark as many as 3,600 bolts in an hour. Although many myths surround the phenomenon, scientists claim it is just regular lightning whose frequency can be explained by regional topography and wind patterns.

The Hottest Place on Earth

https://www.youtube.com/watch?v=GZ6Xp1o9Yfl

Death Valley, California, is the planet's hottest place. The temperature reached a record 134°F on July 10, 1913. The unique geographical and geological makeup of the valley—the lowest place in North America—turns it into a huge oven, sending temperatures above 120°F on numerous occasions. And that's just the air. Ground temperatures often exceed 200°F—hot enough to fry an egg!

The Day the Earth Fell Apart

http://y2u.be/ldsWlf2OSYQQ

A magnitude-9 earthquake shook northeastern Japan in March 2011. It was the most powerful earthquake ever recorded to have hit Japan, and the fourth most powerful earthquake in the world since modern record-keeping began in 1900. It caused a tsunami and a nuclear plant meltdown and moved Japan's main island of Honshu eastward by 8 feet. This compelling video shows what it is like to be caught in the midst of such a terrifying and devastating event.

EXTREME SPORTS RECORDS

There's danger out there on the streets. Especially if you are mad enough to try to go faster, higher, lower than anyone else in your chosen extreme sport.

Sacré Bleu!

http://y2u.be/8CJURZ5HAs4

French athlete Taig Khris is a hero of the inline skating world, but he is as well-known by the French public for skating off tall buildings. Having taken a plunge from the second floor of the Eiffel Tower in 2010, Khris has now jumped from the Sacré-Coeur—the highest point in Paris. He flew down the 492-foot ramp, taking off with the whole city behind him, and soft-landed on an inflatable half pipe. He set a new world distance record with a long jump of 95 feet.

▶ Surf's Up and Up

https://www.youtube.com/watch?v=mLH8OFLclsU

Taking place on International Surfing Day to promote Huntington Beach, California, as *the* Surf City, 66 surf-mad record breakers (between 15 and 79 years old) braved the waters on a supersize (42 feet 1 inch long, 11 feet wide) surfboard—so enormous that it had to be lifted into the sea by a forklift truck—to smash the world record for the most people surfing on the same surfboard. The gang of 66 stayed onboard for an impressive 13 seconds to break the record before wiping out.

◄ Russian BASE Jumper

http://y2u.be/oQjp0DgqWpg

Russian extreme-sports star Valery Rozov endured a 31-day expedition to reach the site of his record-breaking BASE jump. In 2013, he had performed the highest-ever BASE jump on Mount Everest, but that wasn't enough for the adrenaline junkie. In 2016, he climbed to just below the summit of the sixth-highest mountain in the world, Cho Oyu in China, in an attempt to better his record. From a height of over 25,000 feet, Valery leaped off the mountain, spending 90 seconds in free fall before his parachute opened, and landing on a glacier 5,500 feet below and 11,500 feet away.

100-Foot Backflip

http://y2u.be/N93aKejme5I

"I was like, 'Holy moly, I forgot how long I'd be in the air,'" daredevil Cam Zink told ESPN after his monumental 100-foot backflip in California in 2014. "Man, I'm just staring in the sky for like ever." The daredevil hit 46 miles per hour going downhill before he took off on the world's longest dirt-to-dirt mountain bike backflip and then made a perfect landing. Cam compared his 100-foot breakthrough to the 4-minute mile, expecting others to soon take the record farther. We'll see . . .

▼ Backbreaking Work

http://y2u.be/Z-OsL4eCgP0

Records don't just happen. New Zealand's Jed Mildon not only spent three intensive months training for his historic triple BMX backflip, but also had to build a super-ramp, 66 feet high, into a hillside in order to do it. Jed had kept his attempt to become the first-ever rider to perform three full backward rotations secret before attempting it in front of 2,000 spectators. They watched spellbound as he careered down the long ramp, shot up a 11.8-foot super kicker, became airborne, and created history.

▼ Smile and Wave

https://www.youtube.com/watch?v=y9mexETonKA

On a perfect sunny day in June 2015, off the coast of Cavalaire-sur-Mer in the south of France, 58 daredevils, known as "flyboarders," set a new record for the largest water-jetpack flight formation. As extreme seaside spectaculars go, this was a doozy! American flyboard champion Damone Rippy even stunned the huge crowds (on the shore and out at sea) by performing his trademark "Eye of the Storm" double backflip with his jetpack. The video is worth watching for this alone!

LARGEST FORMATION OF WATER JETPACKS

SUPER SPORTS STARS

You don't have to be a big-time pro to be a sporting record breaker. A former NASA scientist, a teenage cheerleader, and 6,000 students all wrote their name in the book in style.

Jumping Schoolboy

http://y2u.be/_2y24qfzxGA

It's jumping—but not as you know it. There are no rhyming songs for 15-year-old Cen Xiaolin to jump along to as he competes in the World Inter School Rope Jumping Championships in Dubai. Well, nobody could sing that fast anyway. The high-school student from China's Guangdong Province clocked up a sensational 110 alternate foot jumps in 30 seconds and 548 in 3 minutes at the championships. The footage is astonishing—it looks sped up and the rope is virtually invisible, but Cen's hands and legs really are moving that fast.

WORLD'S LARGEST DODGEBALL GAME

▼ University Challenge

http://y2u.be/ZdkU4oDcp40

Forget Harvard and Yale or Oxford and Cambridge; the greatest university rivalry is between the University of California, Irvine, and the University of Alberta in Canada. Since 2010, the two colleges have had a running battle to seal the record for the largest dodgeball game. Alberta was the first to make a mark with 1,198 players, but since then the honors have swung back and forth. In 2012, in a game involving 6,084 participants, Irvine took the title, but who knows what the Canadians have planned?

Wet the Baby's Head

http://y2u.be/wBsJcGpZvw0

Zyla can't walk or talk, but she looks pretty comfortable on water skis. Perhaps that's unsurprising, as she's the daughter of champion barefoot water-skier Keith St. Onge and champion show skier Lauren Lane St. Onge, but what is surprising is that she's only six months old. Having seen her take to the specially made "baby ski," which they dragged her around the house on, her mom and dad were confident she could actually ski on water—and they were right. In May 2016, Zyla water-skied on Lake Silver, in Winter

Tumble Turn

http://y2u.be/H4WvgsSSwT0

You may not have heard of Angel Rice but, if power tumbling succeeds in becoming an Olympic sport, she will be a global celebrity. Power tumbling involves momentum and strength in a short series of twists and flips, and the 17-year-old is the United States team's star. Known as the "Queen of Tumbling," Angel has twice won the World Cheerleading Championships, but it has been her TV appearances that have brought her the most attention. After breaking the world record for tumbling in one minute on the *Today* show, she was up to her twisting tricks again with Steve Harvey.

▲ Putting It Right

http://y2u.be/htmbMSRj1SQ

Dave Pelz quit being a NASA scientist in 1976 to concentrate on his golf coaching. Using scientific methods, he became an expert in the "short game"—shots made from within around 100 yards of the hole. In 2004, his research paid off. Filming a TV segment for the Golf Channel during PGA Championship week at Whistling Straits in Kohler, Wisconsin, Pelz holed a 206-foot putt—beating Irish broadcaster Terry Wogan's previous record of 99 feet at Gleneagles in Scotland.

RECORD-
BREAKING
STRIKER

◀ Zlatan's the Man

http://y2u.be/kH56IU1Yrn0

Can British soccer team Manchester United's July 2016 signing of Zlatan Ibrahimovic inspire them to a league title? If anyone can, it is surely Zlatan. The Swedish striker has been a record-breaking phenomenon at his extensive list of former clubs. In addition, he shares the record for winning championships in four countries (Italy, Spain, France, and Holland), has won league titles with more clubs than any other soccer player, and is the only player to score in the UEFA Champions League with six different teams. And, along with Cristiano Ronaldo, he remains the only player to have scored a goal in every minute of a top-flight soccer match.

PURE STRENGTH

You won't see weights being lifted like this down at the local gym. These people pull, flip, and lift in eye-watering feats of strength that just don't seem possible.

What a Waist

http://y2u.be/jcqRPdvb18w

Paul "Dizzy Hips" Blair. His name kind of gives it away, because Paul is a "hulaholic"—a man addicted to spinning hoops around his waist. Among his extensive collection of world records are the most hoops twirling at once from a dead start (132), twirling the largest hula hoop (43 feet), and hula-hooping for the longest distance (1 mile). This video sees him add brute strength to his unquestionable hula-hooping credentials as he secures the record for the heaviest hula hoop by continuously twirling a 100-pound tractor tire around his waist for more than 10 seconds.

Weight of the World

https://www.youtube.com/watch?v=3dJgsJ-DeA4

John Evans, the world's foremost head-balancing strongman, is superhuman. It's a scientific fact. In 2013, the University of Derby in England scanned his 68-year-old body and concluded that his skeleton grows stronger the older he becomes, not weaker, unlike the rest of us. Even before the revelation of his superpowers, Evans smashed a Guinness World Record when, on May 24, 1999, he balanced a small car weighing 352 pounds on his head. A record yet to be challenged.

HEAVIEST CAR BALANCED ON HEAD

THE WOMAN WHOSE STRENGTH IS HER HAIR

▼ Steel Yourself

http://y2u.be/k9rQAOp3xVQ

Amandeep Singh is the Indian Man of Steel—a guy who has immense body strength, seemingly feels no pain, and is surely as mad as a box of frogs. Witness his show reel, where he makes his bid to be known as the World's Strongest Man. It's difficult not to wince as he retains a grip on ropes holding back 20 motorcyclists,

 has a car run over his head, and a full-size truck run over his butt, and takes sledgehammer blows to his most sensitive body parts. Now that's gotta hurt!

Flipping Marvelous

http://y2u.be/4A8Iam4x47E

What do muscle men do when they get old? They start breaking strength records. In 2011, Derek Boyer, 16 times a national champion and the undisputed king of Australian strongmen, was at the end of his career. No worries, pal! Boyer went along to the iconic Outback Festival in Winton, Australia, and broke the world record for flipping a car 10 times. He enjoyed it so much, he went back in 2013 and beat his own record—in a flipping amazing 2 minutes 52 seconds.

▼ Letting Her Hair Down

http://y2u.be/YoBFYQiOCHE

Circus of Horrors star Anastasia IV (Joanna Sawicka from London, England) is proud of her hair. She combs it for hours and washes it five

 times a day. Anastasia isn't vain, she needs to do this to keep her record-breaking hair in top condition. Anastasia spends most of her stage show dangling from her hair, but also lifts record weights with her locks, lifts people, and, in this clip, pulls a 2.5-ton funeral hearse 65 feet 6 inches down the road in under 4 minutes.

▼ Boeing, Boeing, Gone

http://y2u.be/tls-Jli6eQE

Mark Kirsch is the guy you want on your tug-of-war team.
His claims to be the World's Strongest Man of all time look
pretty impressive if this clip is anything to go by. We see
Mark dragging a Boeing 767 along the runway. Yes! Taxiing
a jumbo jet weighing 200,000 pounds with just a rope and
a harness! By hauling the metal monster 100 feet in less than
40 seconds, he set the world record for the heaviest-ever
plane pull.

THE MAN WHO
DRAGGED A
BOEING

BACKWARD RECORDS

Doing something backward is a favorite among record breakers. Sometimes skillful, sometimes dangerous, and often looking silly, our heroes set to their task without fear of neck ache.

◀ Thunder's Back

http://y2u.be/o4fzSkAgNP4

Although it has since been broken, at one point, Thunder Law of the Harlem Globetrotters held the record for the longest-ever basketball shot. And although he has had to give up that crown, he can take solace in an even more incredible achievement: the longest shot facing away from the hoop. His one-handed backward launch propelled the ball 82 feet 2 inches—almost the length of the court and 10 feet farther than the previous record—for a perfect three-pointer.

◢ Parallel Parking

http://youtu.be/VSp1olKp_f0

Try this maneuver when you're faced with a tight parking space at the local grocery store parking lot. In front of a live audience at the 2015 Performance Car Show, British stunt driver Alastair Moffatt slid a Fiat 500 1.2 Cult into the narrowest of parallel-parking spaces. Moffat's magnificent hand-brake turn was made in a standard manual car with an enhanced steering wheel and pumped-up tire pressures. Sliding into a space just 3 inches longer than the car enabled Moffat to reclaim a world record that had been taken from him by a Chinese stunt driver. He bested his rival by less than a quarter of an inch.

Keep Going Bikewards

http://y2u.be/pl5MvRtl89g

Australian Andrew Hellinga learned to ride backward to impress the girls at school, but then put his skills to good use. In a 24-hour challenge for charity, he rode backward for 209 miles. With a unique style of sitting on top of the handlebars and facing backward, Hellinga broke the existing 24-hour record of 112 miles in just 10 hours 15 minutes. After a brief stop to celebrate, he carried on to nearly double the record at an average speed of more than 8.6 miles per hour.

▼ Ramping It Up

http://y2u.be/XUIiffRMfVQ

Ever wondered what skateboarders do for thrills when they grow out of their baggy shorts and elbow pads? Professional skateboarder Rob Dyrdek set 21 different skateboarding records before moving on to be a TV star and all-round entertainer. He broke doughnut-and-banana-eating records on his hit show *Rob & Big*, but once a ramp man . . . In the parking lot of a theme park, Dyrdek reversed his Chevrolet Sonic off one ramp and flew 89 feet 3.25 inches through the air to land cleanly on another. What a guy!

THE WORLD'S LONGEST REVERSE RAMP JUMP

▶ Bowling Backward

http://y2u.be/ex5iwpBHhdw

YouTube has opened up an opportunity for records to be broken all over the world. You no longer need officials and men in blazers to set an authentic record, just a clear video of your achievement. Step forward the most unlikely looking hero in Andrew Cowen of Illinois. Andrew was determined to throw a 300 score (pretty impossible for us weekend bowlers)— while facing the wrong way. He managed 280—two more than the official record—and might have reached his 300 if not for that second frame slipup.

TOTALLY GROSS!

Are you ready to be completely grossed out? These are some of the yuckiest, flesh-creeping, and nauseating clips on the site. And, of course, they are absolutely mesmerizing.

Pardon Me

http://y2u.be/gU3jBonhsrQ

"The goal of the WBF, based in Geneva, is to restore burping to a place of respectability in Western culture and to remove the stigma that has attached itself to this practice during the past millennium." This is how, between hearty belches, a World Burping Federation spokesperson introduced the inaugural World Burping Championships at New York's Hudson Station Bar. This video features the competition's winner, Tim Janus, who set a world record with his 18.1-second-long burp. While happy with his prize, Tim seems eager for burping to become multi-discipline, setting his sights on future records in decibel burping and burp talking.

MILK-SQUIRTING CHAMPION

▶ Squirt Off

http://y2u.be/H7EPl1N_aN4

It's the ultimate squirting-milk-from-the-eye battle! Please don't try this at home. It hurts and can lead to lasting damage to the eyes. Plus, it's altogether a pretty repulsive thing to do. Even so, have a look at these two heroes squirting it out for the record. The trick, apparently, is to snort milk up your nose, close your mouth, block your nostrils, and build up the pressure in the nose. The milk has nowhere else to go but to escape through a duct in the eyes. Yuck!

MOST COCKROACHES HELD IN THE MOUTH

▼ Cockroach Challenge

http://y2u.be/jtXXWz-iKKQ

Even if celebrity reality-TV shows have made you somewhat blasé about the eating of creepy-crawlies, this record by Travis Fessler of Florence, Kentucky, still leaves an uneasy taste in the mouth. Fessler takes on the world record for putting the most Madagascar hissing cockroaches in his mouth. It's enough that he can bear to pick up one of the critters, let alone have room to stuff 11 roaches into his mouth at the same time. Animal lovers can relax: all 11 reappear, looking healthy and as disgusting as ever.

THE MOUTH WITH THE MOST MAGGOTS

◣ Gross Bucket Central

http://y2u.be/p5nqEYakUus

Charlie Bell smashed the record for moving maggots with his mouth without ever even having put one of the disgusting wrigglers between his lips. He'd practiced with rice at home, but was somewhat unprepared for the shock of the smell of the larvae. He told the *Sun* newspaper: "I didn't realize that they would smell so revolting. They do their business in the tubs and so they stink of ammonia. It was like putting my head down a filthy public toilet." Nice.

MULTIPLE RECORD HOLDERS

For some people, breaking one mention in the record books is just not enough. One sniff of glory has them searching for more.

Keepy-Uppy King

http://y2u.be/oFA0JLWgVGY

Until Ashrita (see below) came along, Paul Sahli proudly boasted the "most records" crown. The Swiss juggler—now a senior citizen—was a master foot juggler and still claims 64 world records. Unlike Ashrita, his records vary only in the size of the ball he's juggling: foot juggling a soccer ball for more than 14 hours; a 13-pound medicine ball for 1 hour 6 minutes; and a tennis ball while climbing up a fire ladder for 50 steps.

◄ Record-Breaking Royalty

http://y2u.be/Dj7U8xcnn_0

Ashrita holds the ultimate world record: the record for holding the most records. Born Keith Furman in New York, he was inspired by his spiritual guru to undertake feats of physical endurance. He has set more than 500 official records since 1979 and holds more than 200 existing records, including Fastest Mile Balancing Milk Bottle on Head, Longest Underwater Hula Hooping, Catching Grapes in His Mouth (86 in a minute), and Balancing a Pool Cue on Finger for Longest Distance (8.95 miles).

HOLDER OF THE MOST WORLD RECORDS

📐 Mr. Olympic

http://y2u.be/OK0k6i2d_jk

"This all started with one little dream as a kid to change the sport of swimming and try to do something nobody has ever done," said U.S. swimmer Michael Phelps. Well, he can check off that one on his to-do list. A gold in the men's 4x100 meters medley relay at the 2016 Rio Olympics took Michael Phelps's medal tally to 28 (23 gold, 3 silver, and 2 bronze)—10 more than the next most decorated Olympian, gymnast Larisa Latynina. Despite the announcement of his retirement after the Rio Games, many believe he could be back for more in 2020.

POP'S MOST SUCCESSFUL MUSICIAN

▲ Houston, We Have a . . . Beatle

http://y2u.be/hpvE8kVGeZI

Once a member of the Beatles, Paul McCartney has gone on to become the most successful musician and composer in popular music history. He has a host of sales and radio-play world records, the most Number 1 hits ever, the most frequently covered song in history ("Yesterday" has been sung by more than 4,000 artists), the largest paid audience for a solo concert (350,000 people, in 1989 in Brazil)—and, perhaps best of all, he was the first artist to broadcast live to space.

IMPRESSIVE BUILDINGS

Yes, it's interesting to discover the dates and dimensions of the world's record-breaking buildings, but how much better is it to watch one being built fast—or demolished in seconds? Thank you, YouTube!

Head for Heights

http://y2u.be/a2p4BOGXSBw

Do you have vertigo? If so, maybe you should skip this video. Here, a man known only as "Urban Endeavors" takes us up 1,500 feet, twice the height of the Eiffel Tower, to the very top of the world's tallest TV tower, in North Dakota. The tower itself is an unexceptional structure, but the journey is nail-biting and breathtaking, because our guide climbs without ropes or harness—just gloves and bucketfuls of courage. He even forgoes the "easy way up," climbing the outside of the tower instead of using the ladder in the center.

▶ Mesmerizing Moscow

https://www.youtube.com/watch?v=FS17yy1rlsw

October 2015 saw the Moscow International "Circle of Light" Festival screen the world's largest projected image, which was a dazzling 205,582.33 square feet of video animation, onto the iconic architecture of the Ministry of Defense building in Russia. Thousands of people turned up to be mesmerized by the vivid and vibrant visuals, a display that used 140 powerful Panasonic projectors to illuminate the 50-minute film in HD for all to see. Check it out!

LARGEST PROJECTED IMAGE

▶ A Tilt at the Record

http://y2u.be/UEfeqgXPHPA

Everyone has heard of the Leaning Tower of Pisa, and some have heard of the leaning tower of Suurhusen (which leans a farther 1.22 degrees). However, as of 2010, there is a new leaning king on the block—the Capital Gate in Abu Dhabi. In contrast to the previous record holders, the Capital Gate was intentionally designed to lean. Despite being one of the tallest buildings in the city at 35 stories high, it keels as much as 18 degrees westward—more than four times that of Suurhusen.

▼ To Kingdom Come

http://y2u.be/oiftDBtCFt8

Seattle's Kingdome stadium was only 24 years old when it was blasted to smithereens in 2000. Once heralded as a futuristic marvel, it had grown a reputation as the ugliest stadium in North America. So around 6,000 holes were drilled into the 100,000-ton structure and crammed with dynamite. At a click of a button, they were exploded with detonation cords burning at 24,000 feet per second. In the space of 20 seconds, the city's once-great landmark was leveled to the ground in the world's fastest-ever demolition.

A Building Sight

http://y2u.be/Ps0DSihggio

There are no building workers sitting on the walls eating their lunch and shouting at passersby in this video. They are far too busy erecting the fastest building on the planet. This time-lapse video shows the 30-story Ark Hotel being constructed next to Dongting Lake in Hunan Province, China, in just 15 days, or 360 hours. And this is no shoddily built edifice. All of the structure is soundproofed and thermal-insulated and the hotel is built to withstand a major earthquake.

THE FASTEST DEMOLITION IN HISTORY

▼ Hit the Roof

http://y2u.be/iD4qsWnjsNU

The Khalifa Tower (Burj Khalifa), a skyscraper in
Dubai, is the highest man-made structure in the
world. Unsurprisingly, it has been a target for BASE
jumpers wanting to set records. Two jumpers
created a world record in 2008 when they illegally
jumped from the 160th floor, but this 2014 "official"
jump surpassed that. Fred Fugen and Vince Reffet
leaped from a platform built above the top of the
building, some 2,716 feet 6 inches from the ground.
They actually did it six times to make sure the video
was impressive!

THE
WORLD'S
TALLEST
BUILDING

SUPERFAST RECORDS

The best records are those feats we think we can do pretty well ourselves. Just watch these guys text, clap, or throw a Frisbee—and see if you might match them.

Dressed/Undressed

http://y2u.be/ksymwAItE0M

This one is just for fun. Who would think it was possible to undress in less than a second? The speedy disrober is a Japanese actor and comedian called Herachonpe. His appearance on a Japanese TV show is a feature of many YouTube compilations, because he has a unique way of taking his clothes off. It's got to be a world record, surely, and at the very least, it will raise a smile.

In the Balance

http://y2u.be/bDFZok9uzdk

Try to balance an egg. It isn't easy, they are just not made for it. It would take most people 5 minutes to balance one egg. Back in 2003, Bryan Spotts helped break the record of most eggs balanced at once with 1,290 eggs. But he was hungry for more records, so he invented the category of fastest time to balance a dozen eggs. Finding his record broken, Bryan decided it was time to poach it back—at a shopping mall in Hong Kong.

▼ Happy Clapper

http://y2u.be/ORp2nzwHXN0

His hands are almost a blur, like the wings of a hummingbird, but you can still hear the individual snaps as Bryan Bednarek claps a mighty 804 times in a minute. Bryan is a picture of Zen-like concentration as he keeps up a rhythm of 13 beats a second, his palms meeting to make sure each qualifies as a clap loud enough to register on a nearby monitor. One thing is for sure—he certainly deserves a round of applause.

RECORD-BREAKING HANDCLAPPING

▶ Fstst Txtr in Wrld

http://y2u.be/87GSLXM4lko

Of course the texting record is held by a teenager. But 17-year-old Brazilian Marcel Fenandes Filho is no slacker. He's a physics student who just happens to be nifty with the fingers. Want to try? With perfect spelling and punctuation he texted: "The razor-toothed piranhas of the genera Serrasalmus and Pygocentrus are the most ferocious freshwater fish in the world. In reality they seldom attack a human." In just 18.19 seconds.

▲ Quick on the Draw

http://y2u.be/iS9uGktUCrY

The self-proclaimed Fastest Man with a Gun Who Ever Lived, Bob Munden went to that great shootout in the sky in 2012. He left behind a legend of a gunslinger whose records will never be beaten, and although this is clearly puffed-up myth, there is no doubt he was quick on the draw. It took him just 0.0175 seconds to draw his gun. In his lifetime, Munden set and reset 18 world records for walk and draw; drawing, shooting, and holstering; and for quick-fire accuracy.

Speedy Frisbee

http://y2u.be/TO2RQj-L7gg

Simon Lizotte was a Frisbee prodigy. Dubbed "The Wunderkind," Lizotte, from Bremen in Germany, has dominated the German Disk Golf scene for years. He was the 2012 European Champion and is renowned in the game for his power on the drive. He holds the record for the longest disk throw (863.5 feet—the length of about two and a half football fields), but here he notches up the fastest throw ever recorded at 89.5 miles per hour.

WORLD'S FASTEST GUNSLINGER

SOUND AND VISION

They say it takes all kinds to make a world, but the record world has the strangest inhabitants of all. Call them weird, call them mad; they call themselves "record breakers"!

Rock the World

https://www.youtube.com/watch?v=A8p_AQQ-t38

Wrestler, actor, superstar, and monolith of a man, Dwayne "The Rock" Johnson is an actor who likes to do many of his own stunts. His biggest stunt to date, going for the Guinness World Records title for the most selfies taken in 3 minutes, was also his most grueling! Taken at the world premiere of his movie *San Andreas*, in London's Leicester Square on May 21, 2015, the actor captured 105 selfies with fans who lined up to be a part of the earth-shattering record attempt. How's that for rocking the world?

▶ Heard That Scream Before?

http://y2u.be/cdbYsoEasio

In a 1963 western *The Charge at Feather River*, Private Wilhelm is shot by an arrow. His cry was added using a pained yell that was first recorded for a 1951 Gary Cooper western. The cry, now dubbed "the Wilhelm Scream," was reused in movies for the next 60 years and is the most used sound effect in movie history. Often a movie geeks' in-joke, it appears in low-budget movies as well as multimillion-dollar blockbusters, such as *Star Wars* and *Toy Story*.

007 01

https://www.youtube.com/watch?v=Vd5uELqHyg4

Ever since the first James Bond movie, *Dr. No* in 1962, there has been a string of killer songs to accompany the 007 superspy movies, from the daring "Live and Let Die" by Paul McCartney (1973) to Adele's stirring "Skyfall" (2012). But none of the previous 24 Bond songs have ever gone on to become a UK No. 1. However . . . *Drum roll, please* . . . that honor has now been awarded to Sam Smith's epic ballad of love and regret, "Writing's on the Wall," taken from *Spectre* (2015), which debuted at the top spot in October 2015.

▲ Take the Stage

http://y2u.be/V1U-T_m3kMU

MOST EXPENSIVE STAGE SHOW EVER

The Irish rock band U2 likes records—and not just the musical kind. Their 360° Tour in 2009–10 was not only the highest-grossing tour in history, but it also featured the largest stage and the loudest sound system. In other words, it was the most expensive show ever staged. On each of their 110 dates, Bono and the band played inside a huge arachnid—a 200-ton structure nicknamed "The Claw"—augmented by a million-piece video wall that needed 300 people to assemble. This fascinating time-lapse film captures it all as the supersize stage is put up and taken down again.

CRAZY CRITTERS

There's no such thing as a fair fight in the wild. Clawing, biting, stinging, and kicking are all allowed. These guys are the best in the business.

Angry Bird

http://y2u.be/YA58sS3x2Oo

Hailing from the rain forests of Australia and New Guinea, the cassowary has a bony crest on its head capable of knocking down small trees, and daggerlike sharp claws. Growing up to 6 feet tall and weighing in at more than 130 pounds, it can reach speeds of 30 miles per hour—and is capable of kicking with both legs at the same time. They have gutted dogs, slaughtered horses, and maimed and even killed humans. The most dangerous bird by far.

Sting in the Tail

https://www.YouTube.com/watch?v=xb-0999E6qE

Say hi to *Androctonus australis*—but don't get too close. The creature's name means "southern man-killer" and, indeed, the fat-tailed scorpion, as it is commonly known, is the deadliest scorpion in the world. Found in the deserts of the Middle East and Africa, the venom of the fat-tailed scorpion causes several human deaths every year. The killer critters aren't huge—they grow up to only 4 inches long—but they are often found hiding in the brickwork or concrete cracks of houses. So go careful where you put your fingers!

▶ Packing a Punch

http://y2u.be/ti2Uoc1RXuQ

The mantis shrimp is a fabulous creature. A shrimp-size lobster, it has big bug eyes, comes in dazzling colors, and packs the fastest and strongest punch in the animal kingdom. Sometimes referred to as "thumb splitters," their claws are strong enough to split human appendages, and the shrimp has a punch stronger than a .22-caliber pistol. It has even been known to smash the glass of aquariums when riled. Just watch the slow-motion footage of this champion slugger throwing a right hook!

THE SHRIMP THAT PACKS A PUNCH

▶ Iron Jaws

http://y2u.be/akbpHX0Wbvw

The human bite exerts a pressure of around 120 psi (pounds per square inch). It's enough to chomp through an apple or a piece of toffee. Lions and sharks have jaws that are five times as strong—good for tearing raw flesh apart or ripping through a small boat. But the iron jaws of the animal world belong to the Nile crocodile. These beasts can snap at 2,500 psi (and have reached 6,000 psi), more than twice as much as the feared shark.

▼ Highly Poisonous

http://y2u.be/UETfZLsWWAM

The inland taipan—or the fierce snake, as it is sometimes known—is the most poisonous snake on the planet. It lives in the dry areas of Australia and feeds on small mammals, its venom being especially adapted to kill them effectively. It is an extremely fast and agile snake that can strike with extreme accuracy and almost always releases venom. One drop of its poison can kill around 100 fully grown men in as little as 30–45 minutes if left untreated.

THE WORLD'S MOST DEADLY SNAKE

AMAZING FOOD RECORDS

Groceries—they're not just for eating, you know. You can use them in art, construction, as a pastime—and to break records. Here's some food for thought.

▶ Pumpkin Pride

http://y2u.be/8eQljtg3tAA

This was the moment the pumpkin world had been waiting for: the first-ever one-ton pumpkin, winning farmer Ron Wallace a $10,000 prize. The historical event happened in 2012 at the All New England Giant Pumpkin Weigh-Off, when Wallace's colossal pumpkin was lifted onto the scale by a forklift truck. It topped out at an astounding 2,009 pounds, beating the record set just the previous day by 165 pounds to become the largest fruit ever grown.

Absolutely Ridiculous, Seriously

https://www.YouTube.com/watch?v=L4Y6VVdk2XY

If the quarter pounder at your local burger bar is a little insubstantial for you, take a trip to Mallie's Sports Grill & Bar in Detroit, Michigan. They pride themselves on their "Absolutely Ridiculous Burger," which breaks—and rebreaks—the world record for the largest hamburger commercially available. You'll need to give the restaurant 72 hours' notice and have $2,000 to spare for the 165-pound burger. It takes 22 hours to cook and is served with 15 pounds of lettuce, 30 pounds of bacon, the same amount of tomatoes, and 36 pounds of cheese, all on a 50-pound bun.

THE INCREDIBLE ONE-TON PUMPKIN

THE WORLD'S LARGEST MOSAIC

◀ Coffee Break

http://y2u.be/Kng_LuXl6HI

Albanian artist Saimir Strati's previous work includes mosaic portraits of Leonardo Da Vinci with nails, a galloping horse with toothpicks, and singer Michael Jackson with paintbrushes. This time he made another mosaic—the largest in the world—with a million coffee beans. Strati says he wants his image of a Brazilian dancer, a Japanese drummer, an American country music singer, a European accordionist, and an African drummer to spread the message of: "One world, one family, over a cup of coffee."

▼ Spaghetti Junction

http://y2u.be/v7SgBUq6_qk

Spaghetti Bridge competitions are held in universities around the world as a test for students' knowledge of engineering, physics, and design. The bridges are made of only spaghetti and glue and are tested for how much weight they can sustain before they shatter. The Budapest Technical University has a great reputation for setting records, and it was their students Miklós Vincze and Csaba Jaró who created Hoverla 5. A beautiful and, as it proved, historic construction, it finally collapsed under a weight of 1,257 pounds.

RECORD-BREAKING SPAGHETTI

SUPERSTRENGTH RECORDS

How desperate can you be to get your name in the record books? These record breakers seem to feel no pain as they take one or more of their senses to the limit.

On the Nail

http://y2u.be/W13JvvsKiJM

Extreme-stunts performer "Space Cowboy" calls himself "Australia's most prolific record breaker"—and with good reason. He has more than 40 records to his name (which is really Chayne Hulttgren), including pulling 906 pounds by fishhooks in his eye sockets for the farthest distance, the fastest arrow caught blindfolded, and most chainsaw-juggling catches on a unicycle. In 2012, the Cowboy displayed his skills on the TV Show *Australia's Got Talent*. Lying on a bed of more than 100 sharp, 8-inch nails, he was driven over by 20 motorcycles in 2 minutes.

FASTEST WALNUT-CRACKER

◀ Nut Job

http://y2u.be/mkgDDCMKXXc

Most of us struggle to crack an English walnut with a pair of metal nutcrackers, but not Pakistani Mohammad Rashid. The martial arts expert just uses his forehead—aiming a well-judged headbutt at a nut the size of a billiards ball. It takes an estimated force of 250 psi (pounds per square inch) to crack a nut, but Rashid works his way through an incredible 155 nuts in just one minute— literally smashing the previous record of 44 walnuts. If I were you though, I'd stick with the nutcrackers—even Rashid finished with a few drops of blood on his head.

▶ A Nose-Blowing Champ

http://y2u.be/6LGiq717r9Q

The 23-year-old Jemal Tkeshelashvili is capable of inflating hot-water bottles to the point of bursting—with his nose! These rubber bottles require ten times more air pressure to inflate than a party balloon, so Jemal needs great lung capacity and the ability to push the air out of his nostrils with incredible force. Here, in 2009, in his hometown of Tblisi, Georgia, he blew up and exploded three hot-water bottles in 23 seconds, including one being sat on by an adult.

THE MAN WITH A CHAMPION NOSE

Thigh High

http://y2u.be/TN59gYxa2to

The sport of crushing fruit between your thighs probably won't threaten the popularity of football on TV any time soon, but Olga Liaschuk's appearance on British TV show *This Morning* caused somewhat of a stir. Seated on a mat in the studio, and watched over by genial show hosts Phillip Schofield and Holly Willoughby, Olga crushed three watermelons between her thighs in just 14 seconds. Ukrainian Olga is also a champion in the perfectly respectable sport of weightlifting, but who wants to watch that when you can see exploding melons?

▼ Game of Throwing

http://y2u.be/MdcnUdzab7E

"I'd be a bloody fool if he didn't frighten me. He's freakish big and freakish strong and quicker than you'd expect for a man of that size." So says Bronn in the smash TV series *Game of Thrones* of the character played by impressive record breaker Hafþór Júlíus Björnsson. "The Mountain," as the 6-foot 6-inch, 405-pound giant is known in the TV series, also goes under the moniker Thor when he's competing in the World's Strongest Man competition. So, finally, we come to his record: A pretty impressive feat of throwing a 33-pound keg over 23 feet in the air.

Table Manners

http://y2u.be/MC6tgknKPQE

Even among strongmen challenges, some records push the boundaries of the bizarre. Take Georges Christen, a national hero in Luxembourg. In a career spanning more than 30 years, Georges has made a name for himself setting records pulling trucks, buses, and ships, and even making a huge Ferris wheel turn—all using his teeth. This performance—a repeat of another record-breaking feat—is a little more special. It shows a woman sitting on a table being carried in the air by Georges—yep, you've guessed it—in his teeth! She seems like a willing participant, but keep an eye on her expression.

HOLDING OUT FOR A HERO

This awesome selection illustrates just how wide-ranging the record-breaking heroes are. Some rely on physical endurance, others on know-how, and some just collect crazy stuff!

◀ Room on the Back

http://y2u.be/6qRzC95YpSE

Plumber Colin Furze's project began in his mom's yard with a normal 125cc scooter, which the ingenious engineer adapted with a homemade aluminum frame, adding 25 seats and extending it to 72 feet—nearly as long as a tennis court. To set the record, Furze had to ride the bike for 328 feet, but he actually rode it for more than a mile. "When I first got on it, I thought it would never work, and at a slow speed it's almost impossible to keep upright," says Colin, but on Saltby Airfield in Grantham, England, he managed a pretty impressive 35 miles per hour.

THE MOST VALUABLE COLLECTION OF HAIR

▶ Hair Today . . .

http://youtu.be/NvILbEoUu0c

John Reznikoff's most prized possession is a frame containing a couple of strands of black hair. They were taken from Abraham Lincoln on his deathbed, and he estimates they are worth $500,000. Reznikoff has the largest collection of celebrity hair in the world, including locks from: King Charles I; Neil Armstrong, the first man on the moon; Marilyn Monroe; and even singed locks of Michael Jackson. If *Jurassic Park*-style DNA "reincarnations" ever become reality, John could have some interesting dinner parties.

▼ Micro Motor

http://youtu.be/6GBwWodOls0

This clip tells the story of British inventor Perry Watkins's attempt to build the world's smallest legally road-worthy car. Using the bodywork of a children's toy car and the chassis and engine of a quad bike, Watkins engineered a hilarious-looking vehicle that was 41 inches high, 26 inches wide, 52 inches long, and capable of traveling at 37 miles per hour. Just about squeezing into the driver's seat, he was able to take it for a spin—even if he did have to ignore the laughter of other drivers.

THE WORLD'S SMALLEST CAR ON THE ROAD

Gym Hero

http://youtu.be/LzciOAhto78

The plank is a favorite exercise for the gym bunnies. With muscles rippling, they lie horizontally, supported by only their forearms and toes. Some even manage to hold the position for a minute or two. So, here's Chinese police officer Mao Weidong in 2014. A member of the SWAT team fighting organized crime, Weidong held the excruciating position for 4 hours 26 minutes, more than an hour past the previous record. He only stopped because it matched his wife's birthday on April 26. A tough man and a romantic, too!

THE LONGEST PLANK EVER HELD

How Low Can You Go

http://y2u.be/AaPtiFO-NLc

Tim Storms goes deep for his record. He's no diver, but singer Tim holds the world record for reaching the lowest note. Due to his oversize vocal chords, Tim can hit notes so low that only huge animals, such as elephants, can hear them. He has reached a G-7 or 0.189Hz—a note eight octaves below the lowest G on the piano (a whole piano length lower). This gives him another record—the greatest vocal range. He has a full 12 octaves, but Tim has warned he could break records again as his voice continues to get lower with age.

TOTALLY DIFFERENT

The record breaker can never stop to ask why. Thankfully, these record setters never questioned putting themselves in harm's way by playing a silly instrument or building a huge chocolate train.

Comfort Blanket

WORLD'S LARGEST CROCHET BLANKET

https://www.youtube.com/watch?v=qK7RYDGj_xk

In February 2016, Mother India's Crochet Queens in Chennai, India, made the largest crochet blanket in the world. How big is it? It's massive! Measuring 120,001 square feet, the blanket covered an entire football field! Creating such a snuggly object took more than 1,000 participants (between 8 and 85 years old) from more than 14 countries hours and hours to create individual 40 x 40-inch sections, which were then sewn together to make one ultra-cozy blanket. After the record was verified, the blanket was deconstructed and the sections were donated to local charities.

▼ Choco Choo Choo

http://y2u.be/Fd2pW0SjWLY

The highlight of Brussels Week of Chocolate in 2012 was a creation by Maltese master chocolatier Andrew Farrugia. His chocolate train was 111.7 feet long and was made of 2,833 pounds of chocolate. Officially the World's Largest Chocolate Structure, it had a locomotive and seven wagons, modeled on different-era Belgian train cars, and included one with a bar and restaurant. Big enough for the most dedicated chocoholic, it contained more than six million calories!

RECORD-BREAKING CHOCOLATE SCULPTURE

◄ Raw Geometry

http://y2u.be/C7XY-HvNWas

In the summer of 2016, sushi mosaics were trending on Instagram. Hundreds of pictures showed sushi squares, artistically arranged in colorful geometric patterns. It is a quintessentially Japanese art form—they are exquisite, delicate, and precise—so, naturally, the world record for the largest sushi mosaic was set in . . . Norway and was created by a chef who runs a sushi bar in Sweden. The mosaic, displayed at the Aspmyra Stadion, in Bode, Norway, measured an incredible 608 square feet and included almost 1,800 pounds of salmon, around 900 pounds of rice, 44 gallons of rice vinegar, 1,060 pounds of cucumber, and 22 pounds of chives.

WORLD'S LARGEST SuSHI MOSAIC

► Take a Bow—or Two

http://youtu.be/mPni3__sWus

Perhaps no one pointed out to Ukrainian musician Oleksandr Bozhyk that when a piece of music says it is a concerto for four violins, that does not mean they all have to be played by the same person. At a live concert in Lviv, Ukraine, in 2012, the virtuoso violinist took up two bows and four violins and proceeded to play—pretty well considering—the soundtrack from the movie *Requiem for a Dream*. It was, of course, the most violins ever played by one person at the same time.

THE MOST VIOLINS IN ONE GO

COOL CAT RECORDS

There is plenty of kitten action and a lot of celebrity cats on YouTube, but not many make the record books. Here's a select few who are on the road to purr-fection.

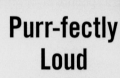

LOUDEST MEOW ON A CAT

Purr-fectly Loud

https://www.youtube.com/watch?v=tFUIVRLXD68

Everyone loves looking at supercute videos of cats online, but this record-breaking kitty is probably the cutest one of all time. Merlin, a rescue cat from Torquay, England, has been tonally fluttering loud and proud after being confirmed as the loudest-purring kitty in the world!

On April 2, 2015, he registered a deafening 67.8 decibels, the same loudness as a busy city street. When it comes to nominative determinism and purring, Merlin is indeed magic!

Fluffy Sweater

http://y2u.be/66pMRSlgle0

Alley, a stray cat, was adopted after she was found looking frail and nervous in a city side street. Taken in by Chicagoan Samantha Martin, Alley had really landed on her feet, because Samantha is a trainer for the traveling cat circus Acro-cats (search for their videos on YouTube—they're really fun), and she quickly discovered that Alley loved to bounce around the platforms she used to teach her cats to jump. As Samantha began to train her, it became apparent that Alley had a real aptitude for jumping, leaping over 6 feet. Could this street cat really become record-breaking royalty?

▶ The Pocket-Size Kitty

http://y2u.be/1vdVRuqQUb4

Singapura are nicknamed "Velcro cats" because of their sometimes irritating desire to stay close to their owners. They have been acknowledged as the smallest breed of cat in the world. The full-grown males reach only around 7 pounds, while females can weigh a paltry 4 pounds. Some claim they were originally river or "drain" cats in Singapore, while others have suggested they were a cross between Abyssinian and Burmese breeds.

THE WORLD'S SMALLEST CAT

▶ Fat Cat

http://youtu.be/7dVn7KNP0co

Garfield is one of the great cartoon cats, right up there with Tom, Top Cat, and Sylvester. Now, there is a real-life Garfield, who shared some of his animated namesake's gargantuan appetite and indolence. Garfield was brought to an animal rescue in Long Island, New York, after his owner passed away, and he shocked the volunteers with his obesity. He tipped the scales at 40 pounds—an average cat weighs around 10 pounds—and earned the distinction of being the fattest cat in the world.

THE WORLD'S FATTEST CAT

◢ Big Big Cat

http://youtu.be/xBznm54nVMM

There are cats, big cats, and then there are ligers. Ligers are the offspring of a male lion and a tigress—huge animals that do not exist in the wild and are only bred in captivity. Hercules, who usually lives at the Myrtle Beach Safari wildlife preserve in South Carolina, is the biggest of them all. He is 6 feet tall, 12 feet long, and weighs 900 pounds—as big as his parents combined. He may look a handful, but his keepers say he's a real pussycat.

THE WORLD'S LARGEST LIGER

CRAZY CROWD RECORDS

Whoever said "Three's a crowd" wasn't in the record-breaking business. To register in the record books, you need great organization, silly costumes, and people by the thousands.

▼ Who You Gonna Call?

http://yt.vu/dqQCj7WKNgk

"Ghostbusters of the world, gear up!" went the call to arms from Paul Feig, director of the 2016 version of the 1984 supernatural horror-comedy classic. The fans responded and 263 people got their ghost on—dressed up as the movie's famous "no-ghost" logo—and gathered at Singapore's Marina Bay Sands to celebrate the launch of the all-female reboot of the *Ghostbusters* movie. Star of the movie Melissa McCarthy was also in attendance and in high spirits as the assembly claimed the title of "Largest gathering of people dressed as ghosts at a single venue."

Very Sweaty Record

https://www.youtube.com/watch?v=pe3WHt-PVKk

Becoming increasingly popular all around the globe, Zumba is currently the hottest, sweatiest exercise class you can think of. Combining dance and aerobics, as well as elements of choreography from hip-hop, soca, samba, salsa, merengue, and mambo music, Zumba is a great way to look cool while getting hot. On July 19, 2015, in the city of Mandaluyong in the Philippines, precisely 12,975 Zumbaholics started dancing in the street to take part in the largest Zumba class in the world, smashing the previous world record and getting a great workout as well!

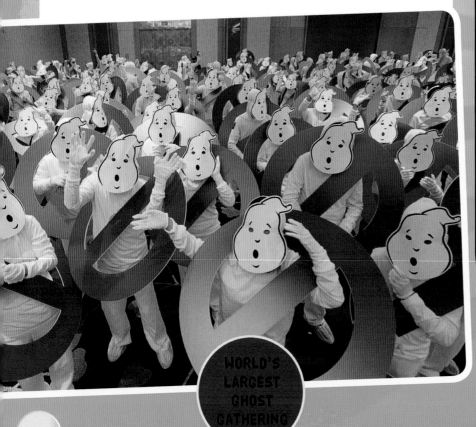

WORLD'S LARGEST GHOST GATHERING

Snow Joke

http://yt.vu/l2vdLCLkUHQ

When you think of Siberia in northern Russia, the first thing that comes to mind isn't beach wear. A region famous for its freezing winters, where temperatures can fall as low as -40°F, it certainly seems an unlikely location for a gutsy record attempt on the world's largest downhill ride in swimsuits. At least the sun was shining in April 2015, when 1,835 skiers and snowboarders, without a care for hypothermia or even chilblains, donned their itsy-bitsy teenie-weenie bikinis and tight-fitting swim briefs to take to the slopes of the region's Mount Zelyonaya's Sheregesh ski resort.

▶ Flying the Flag

http://y2u.be/f04vc_m3gvQ

India's rivalry with Pakistan is often hostile but, in December 2014, the stakes were raised when India stole the world record for the largest human flag from their neighbors. More than 50,000 volunteers began gathering at 5:00 a.m. in the YMCA ground in Chennai, but it wasn't until noon that they were in position to form the tricolor flag. Pakistan's previous record was just short of 29,000—they've probably already started working on recapturing the title.

▼ Ever So Elfish

http://y2u.be/lu8dsjoW5-o

Nearly 2,000 of Santa's little helpers, between the ages of 9 and 15, put on red, green, and white hats, matching T-shirts, and pointy plastic elf ears, and formed up outside a shopping mall in Bangkok. Those participating were required to stand still for 10 minutes with their elf ears and hats on. Some didn't make it and others were disqualified for not putting on their elf ears, but 1,792 correctly attired and standing were still enough to set a new record.

RECORD-BREAKING NuMBER OF ELVES

RECORD-BREAKING DOGS

It's dog beat dog in the competition for canine records. You'll love these proud pooches as they show off their record-breaking skills.

◀ Ugly Mutt

http://youtu.be/7AkYSGllKTk

Two-year-old Peanut, a mutt who is suspected of being a Chihuahua/Shitzu mix, doesn't have a lot going for him. He was seriously burned as a puppy and lived in an animal shelter for nine months before he found a home. On the looks side, he has matted hair, protruding teeth, and looks as much rodent as canine. However, Peanut found fame in California in 2014. In a hotly contested competition, he swept the floor with the other hideous hounds and was crowned the World's Ugliest Dog.

THE UGLIEST DOG IN THE WORLD

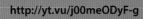

Bursting with Joy

http://yt.vu/j00meODyF-g

If there was ever a dog Olympics, the balloon-popping event would surely be up there with toy hiding and squirrel chasing. Dashing about a room full of balloons with paws, claws, and teeth has athleticism, skill, excitement, and is absolutely hilarious. Here's the current record owner showing how it's done. Jack Russell terrier Twinkie, whose mother, Anastacia, held the title for seven years until 2015, focuses hard and pops 100 balloons in just 39.08 seconds. That's 2.5 balloons per second—no wonder she looks pleased with herself. Give that dog a bone!

BEST SKATEBOARDING DOG

Shot Stopper

http://yt.vu/y55tYGOuqfI

Like all good keepers, Purin stands tall, remains focused, and keeps his paws outstretched. Yes, paws, because Purin, from Chiba in Japan, has set a new world record for the most balls caught by a dog with its paws in one minute. Practice makes perfect for the petite pooch, who spends 15 minutes every day perfecting her catching technique with proud owner Makoto. Purin, however, is no one-trick canine, because she also holds the record for the fastest 33 feet traveled on a ball by a dog, which you can also see on YouTube.

▲ Dog on Wheels

https://www.youtube.com/watch?v=EVnzXA9b7Ww

On November 8, 2015, in Lima, Peru, Otto the bulldog became an overnight Internet sensation . . . and a world-record holder! The three-year-old canine wonder successfully completed the longest human tunnel traveled through by a skateboarding dog—and he made it look so simple, too. Skating underneath the butts of 30 humans—without contact or assistance, and in front of a huge crowd cheering him on—Otto navigated through all the legs with ease and glided smoothly into the record books. This video has now been watched more than two million times, too!

THE WORLD'S SMALLEST DOG

▲ Pocket-Size Pooch

http://youtu.be/fTEIdAyYkac

Like many dogs, Heaven Sent Brandy, the Chihuahua from Florida, is not allowed on the furniture. In her case, it's just because if she jumps off, she'd break a bone. Measuring just 6 inches from tail to nose, the adorable four-year-old is no bigger than a can of cola and is the world's smallest dog in terms of length. She's a nervous little creature—but who can blame her, when every hulking great human in sight wants to cuddle her?

ENDURING PASSION

Breaking records can require years of grooming, hundreds of hours of practice, meticulous arrangement, or serious organization skills. And some just happen in an instance of pure chance.

▶ Bricking It

https://www.youtube.com/watch?v=ZgrsJcuDCD0

Played online by millions of gamers of all ages, Minecraft is a global phenomenon. The world set within a world, where you can create and build anything you can think of, has led to an influx of experts vlogging on YouTube to pass on their essential tips to fellow players. One such pro, Kurt J. Mac, a 33-year-old from Phoenix, Arizona, was awarded a world-record title in September 2015 for the Longest Journey in Minecraft, an honor that has meant walking more than 2,097,152 blocks (the equivalent of 1,304 miles) in four years. Some have estimated that it will take Kurt another 20 years to reach his ultimate destination, the fabled Far Lands, but he remains true to his vision quest: "Minecraft's creator, Notch, said it would be impossible to reach the Far Lands," the online adventurer said. "So I took that as a challenge!"

LONGEST JOURNEY IN MINECRAFT

▼ Heavy Metal

http://yt.vu/5UrG-hY8kUc

Frenchman Michel Lotito is honored with having the strangest recorded diet and it is fair to say that he didn't earn the nickname "Monsieur Mangetout" ("Mr. Snowpea") without tucking into a few odd items. As a child, Lotito experienced pica, a type of compulsive disorder in which people eat nonfood items. Developing his affliction into an act, he went on to devour beds, television sets, bicycles, and shopping carts. His *pièce de résistance* was a Cessna 150 airplane, which took him two years to consume. Lotito died of natural causes in 2007, having partaken of almost 9 tons of metal in his lifetime.

▶ Never Too Old

http://yt.vu/iD7D8BY2d1c

You're never too old to start exercising. That's what we can learn from athlete Charles Eugster, the 200-meter indoor-dash record holder—in the 95-years-and-over category. The former dentist was born in London, England, in 1919 and, having started rowing at 63 and taken up bodybuilding at the age of 87, running was a natural progression for him, although he was 95 before he took to the track. A self-confessed "hopeless runner" in his younger days, after a short training period, Eugster was soon outshining the elite in his age category. His time, by the way, was 55.48 seconds.

THE LARGEST GATHERING OF WALDOS

▲ Where's Waldo?

http://y2u.be/Chnui_Jqxb8

In the best-selling book *Where's Waldo?* (known as *Where's Wally?* in Great Britain and often given other names around the world), readers have to find the character dressed in a red-and-white shirt and hat and black-rimmed eyeglasses. You won't have any difficulty finding him in this clip. More than 3,500 adults, children, and even dogs turned out in Merrion Square in Dublin, Ireland, dressed in Waldo outfits. They managed to set a new world record for the number of people dressed as the popular children's literary character.

On the Fiddle

http://yt.vu/PA_1oS8Ch4U

Record holder Ben Lee is no novelty violinist. He was a child prodigy; a student at the London School of Music; played with the Arctic Monkeys, McFly, and others; and eventually formed the successful rock violin duo Fuse. In the summer of 2009, Lee suffered damage to his right hand and wrist after being run over by a truck while cycling. To inspire his rehabilitation, his bandmate challenged him to break the world record for fastest violinist. In fact, he went on to break the record five times, on both acoustic and electric violin.

AMAZING ATHLETES

All around the world, athletes love to break records, no matter what sport they excel at. These stars are no different, and they have some pretty amazing achievements to crow about.

Surface Tension

http://yt.vu/Vox9KOxC1ZA

The world record for the 50-meter backstroke stands at 24.04 seconds, but an American, Hill Taylor, can claim to have swum it a whole second faster than that. The time set by the Texan-born phenomenon known as "Dolphin Man" was ignored because he swam the whole lap without taking a single stroke. As the swimmers rise on 15 meters (as stated in the rules) to begin their classic backstrokes, Hill Taylor never surfaces, preferring to swim underwater. Demolishing the field, he surges ahead using a combination of a unique streamlined position and an amazingly powerful dolphin kick.

▼ To Me . . . to You . . . to Me

http://y2u.be/p9XkigqHIBg

Mima Ita was a Japanese table tennis prodigy. When just 10 years old, she became the youngest person to win a match at the Japanese senior table tennis championships. Here she is—still only at the age of 11—on the set of the Japanese TV show *100 Handsome Men and Beautiful Women* hitting the ball with metronomic precision 180 times across the table—the most table tennis counter hits ever. Now in her teens, Ita has embarked on a successful table tennis career.

YOUNGEST
TABLE
TENNIS
CHAMPION

▶ Lucky Kick

http://y2u.be/_Zi_uCcfA8s

Seeing a goalkeeper score is one of soccer's rarest sights. When the ball was passed back from the kickoff to English team Stoke City's goalkeeper Asmir Begovic (an international player from Bosnia and Herzegovina), his intention wasn't to join the small band of keeper scorers. However, with just 13 seconds gone on the clock, his upfield kick caught the wind and bounced over opposite number Artur Boruc into the Southampton team's net. It was the sixth-fastest goal in Premier League history but, more important, at 301 feet, it was the longest in competitive soccer in the world.

▼ Jump at the Chance

http://y2u.be/kPZvtlDLjpl

This is an unofficial world record, but there appears no reason to doubt it—and it is exceptional. It features American Kevin Bania, a CrossFit athlete. (CrossFit is a sport featuring weightlifting, sprinting, and jumping exercises.) Bania attempts a record standing box jump, which involves jumping onto a box or level surface. From a standing start, he leaps from the floor to a platform 5 feet 4.5 inches high. Bania himself stands 5 feet 10 inches tall, so he is within 6 inches of jumping his own height.

THE MAN WHO JUMPS ALMOS AS HIGH AS HIMSELF

WILD SPORTS

Terrified by the high board at the swimming pool? Dizzy on the top story of the multistory car park? Then perhaps you should just sit down and watch some who know no fear . . .

▼ New Ball Game

http://y2u.be/NehU-6NCBco

Zorbing is the sport of rolling down a hill in the kind of plastic sphere given to bored hamsters. Protected by a pocket of air between them and the edges of the ball, the participants can thrust the ball forward but have limited control over the direction. Miguel Ferrero from Spain, nicknamed "The Adventurer," was encased in a Zorb ball and threw himself down a ski run at La Molina in the Pyrenees. He reached a record speed of 31.2 miles per hour.

THE FASTEST ZORBING ON RECORD

◄ Extreme Swimming

http://y2u.be/IJY8VgmvXHc

Diane Nyad became the first person to swim the 100 miles from Cuba to Florida without a protective shark cage. Braving rough seas, the fear of shark attack, vomiting from salt-water intake and wearing a heavy suit to withstand jellyfish stings, Diane succeeded on her fifth attempt over 35 years—her fourth since turning 60.

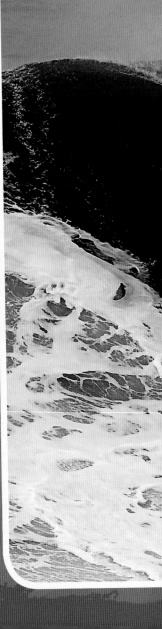

Snow Business

http://yt.vu/f0mTTmOuvUQ

France's Edmond Plawczyk had waited a long time to reclaim his snowboarding speed record. He had originally set the world record in 1997, but that was broken in 1999. April 2015 was payback time as Edmond donned his strange-looking red winged suit and aerodynamic helmet at the top of the slopes of the famous Chabrières piste in the French Alps. He was soon flying down the 4,600-foot course, which at one point measured a gradient of 98 percent, to realize his ambition and a new record speed of 126.309 miles per hour.

▼ Surf's Up and Up

http://y2u.be/dtVQJCq2cCM

Surfing legend Garrett McNamara caught a towering 100-foot wave off the coast of Nazare in Portugal. Risking being slammed into a reef or the ocean floor, he beat his own record by 1 foot. That too was set off Nazare, where an underwater canyon generates some of the world's biggest waves. "You are just going so fast," McNamara told ABC Television. "And you're just chattering, flying down this bumpy, bumpy mountain. Your brain is getting rattled. Your whole body is getting rattled."

THE LARGEST WAVE EVER SURFED

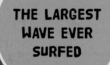

TRULY REMARKABLE

It's a wonderful record-breaking world and YouTube contributors across the globe are out filming every remarkable event and achievement.

Octomum

http://youtu.be/04g4HPdQWZU

Nadya Suleman has patented the name "Octomum." It is just one of many ways she has attempted to earn the money to look after her family. She has 14 children, including the eight born together—the most babies delivered at a single birth to survive. Having given birth to the octuplets in January 2009, Nadya has rarely been out of the media since. She has been criticized for fertility treatment, for taking inappropriate employment, and for claiming welfare benefits—but continues to care for the children.

▼ Pop-Up Painting

http://youtu.be/RwtWZd-sbMc

In June 2014, world-famous Chinese artist Yang Yongchun unveiled a special piece of art. Named *Rhythms of Youth*, it depicted the impressive architectural landscape of Nanjing and the Yangtze River that runs through it. Not only was it the largest and longest street painting in the world, measuring an astonishing 1,200 feet long and covering 28,000 square feet, but it was also an anamorphic painting—created in a distorted manner to make it appear three-dimensional.

THE LONGEST STREET PAINTING

▶ Light It Up

https://www.youtube.com/watch?v=tt0o7cuKY4E

If you're in the mood for some festive cheer, then head on over to Canberra, Australia, and check out David Richards's—known locally as "Christmas Lights Man"—Technicolor display of the light fantastic. Officially recorded as the world's largest display of Christmas lights on an artificial tree, Richards spent hours putting up precisely 518,838 lights to earn the title, even going so far as to top the tree with a 59-inch-tall star that alone contains 12,000 bulbs!

LARGEST DISPLAY OF CHRISTMAS TREE LIGHTS

▼ Water Colors

http://y2u.be/OZwAbQ8iv_A

Jesper Kikkenborg is a Danish marine biologist and artist. Combining both his fields of expertise, he produced a painting at the Blue Planet Aquarium in Denmark. This was no ordinary painting, though: Kikkenborg wore scuba-diving gear and painted his picture inside the 4-million-liter Ocean Tank. Named *Mother Ocean*, it featured eagle rays, hammerhead sharks, and other exotic fish. It took him 23 hours over nine days and measures 48 square feet—the largest underwater painting ever.

A Real Blast

http://yt.vu/iail1vqS4MM

The best firework displays always keep something special back for the grand finale of the show. The display for the Feast of St. Catherine in Zurrieq, Malta, certainly didn't disappoint. The crowds that had gathered at one of the island's biggest festivals witnessed the spectacle of the world's single biggest firework. The rocket, called the *ballun tal-blalen* (which loosely translates as "balloon of balls"), exploded from a 10-foot-wide shell weighing 570 pounds, launching a chain reaction that saw the whole sky covered in chrysanthemum-pattern lights. Enjoy—it may not last long, but the brief effect is completely dazzling.

THE
HIGHEST-
EVER LEGO
TOWER

▼ Tower Power

http://y2u.be/KuQkUmz9fmY

They might make film heroes now but, for years, Lego bricks were purely for construction. Thankfully, some are still preserving the art of the interlocking brick. In the shadow of St. Stephen's Basilica in Budapest, children, locals, and Danish engineers constructed the highest-ever Lego tower. Rising 114 feet, the towering spire was made of 450,000 colorful bricks and appropriately topped with another great toy—the Rubik's Cube, a puzzle designed by a Hungarian professor of architecture, Ernő Rubik.

IT TAKES ALL KINDS

Isn't it a wonderful record-breaking world when a twerking champion and a pair of extreme cyclists can share a page with one of the greatest soccer players ever?

▼ Hard Twerk

http://youtu.be/otZmEyIDGsY

After Miley Cyrus's twerking at the 2013 MTV Video Music Awards, New Orleans rapper Big Freedia went about reclaiming the dance. The self-proclaimed Queen of Bounce claimed twerking had been started by the "bounce" dance scene of New Orleans. So, in her hometown, Big Freedia—Freddie Ross's stage name—cued her hit "Duffy," and led a world record 410 dancers, ranging from the age of 8 to 80, as they shook their rumps for two continuous minutes.

CHAMPION TWERKING IN NEW ORLEANS

▼ Everybody Freeze!

http://yt.vu/BrfN_o91Igg

Fall 2016 and a new craze was sweeping the Internet: the Mannequin Challenge. Across numerous platforms, people shared videos of groups acting as if they had been frozen in time. Perhaps the most famous video came from the White House and featured Bruce Springsteen, Tom Hanks, Diana Ross, and others (you can view it on YouTube). Of course, competition for the biggest Mannequin Challenge was soon on, with pride of place going to this magnificent effort by 55,000 spectators, players, staff, and paramedics at a Cape Town sevens rugby tournament in South Africa's Cape Town Stadium.

WORLD'S LARGEST MANNEQUIN CHALLENGE

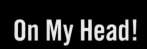

On My Head!

http://y2u.be/joA086aXDlk

As a Nigerian soccer player in Cambodia, the possibility existed that Harrison Chinedu might have got overlooked by the national team's coaches. But Harrison was hard to miss when, wearing the national soccer kit, he rode a bicycle from a beach outside Nigeria's capital of Lagos all the way into the city to the national stadium. Oh, did I forget to say that he did the whole 64 miles balancing a soccer ball on his head? Six months earlier, his record walk with a ball on his head (28.84 miles) had been quickly broken, so this time he's hoping he's in the record books to stay.

On Your Bike!

https://www.youtube.com/watch?v=k-NpZQIQ6pE

Members of the Dutch cycling organization Mijl Van Mares Werkploeg were so desperate to break a world record, they built the longest bicycle in the world, measuring an eye-watering 117 feet 5 inches long. The bicycle has to be operated by two people: one steers at the front while the other pedals from the back. When asked if riding the bike was as easy as riding any other, the man behind the record, Frank Pelt, answered, "Yes . . . just don't turn any corners!"

▼ Pulling Faces

http://y2u.be/72NW0pobAnw

Tang Shuquan of Chengdu City, China, spends a lot of time hoping the wind doesn't change direction and he stays "like that." Named the King of Deformed Faces, Tang spent ten years working on being able to contort his face into the ugliest shapes possible. After winning the world record for gurning, Tang, who has the extraordinary ability of biting his own nose, even challenged all-comers—offering a 100,000 yuan ($15,850) prize to anyone who can match his face-stretching skills.

THE GURNING WORLD CHAMPION

MAD MOVIE RECORDS

Roll the credits! From Bollywood to Hollywood, the glamorous and exciting world of the movies lists the famous and the not so famous in its annals of achievement.

◀ Titanic Record

http://youtu.be/2e-eXJ6HgkQ

The 1997 movie *Titanic* starring Leonardo DiCaprio and Kate Winslet was, at the time, the most expensive movie ever made. It was worth it. *Titanic* became the most successful movie ever in terms of box-office and critical success. It has the most Oscar nominations (14, tied with *All About Eve*) and the most Academy Awards (11, tied with *Ben-Hur*) and is the second-highest-grossing movie ever (*Avatar* is first), having taken more than $2.2 billion at the box office.

AN EXPENSIVE RECORD BREAKER

A Dress to Impress

http://yt.vu/RPW3kavkoFQ

On May 19, 1962, during the forty-fifth birthday celebrations for President John F. Kennedy, actress Marilyn Monroe sashayed onto the stage at Madison Square Garden, took off her fur coat, and famously sang "Happy Birthday, Mr. President." Under that fur coat, Marilyn was wearing a sheer, sequined dress so tight that she had to be sewed into it. It was an era-defining moment. Fast-forward 54 years, and that same dress is under the hammer at auction. It was bought by Ripley's Believe It or Not for an incredible $4.8 million, making it the most expensive dress ever.

▲ Selfie Aggrandizement

http://youtu.be/GsSWj51uGnl

This was the picture that appeared on millions of phones and tablets after Ellen DeGeneres posted it on Twitter during the Eighty-Sixth Annual Academy Awards in 2014. The most retweeted message ever (more than three million times to date), the selfie featured Hollywood stars Jared Leto, Jennifer Lawrence, Channing Tatum, Meryl Streep, Julia Roberts, Kevin Spacey, Brad Pitt, Lupita Nyong'o, Angelina Jolie, Peter Nyong'o Jr., and Bradley Cooper, who took the photo. Ellen's comment on the tweet read: "If only Bradley's arm was longer. Best photo ever. #oscars"

Extra Special

http://youtu.be/miuzO4yI0V4

Acclaimed director Richard Attenborough faced a real challenge when filming *Gandhi* on location in India in 1980. He was determined to re-create the great man's life as accurately as possible and had to film a funeral scene in which a million people had lined the route. Attenborough chose to film on the thirty-third anniversary of Gandhi's funeral and managed to recruit around 300,000 volunteers and actors—the most extras ever to appear in a feature movie.

THE MOST RETWEETED MESSAGE EVER

Feel the Force

https://www.youtube.com/watch?v=sGbxmsDFVnE

In December 2015, *Star Wars: The Force Awakens* became the fastest movie in history to earn $1 billion at the global box office, taking just 12 days to achieve its historic haul. The movie, which cost more than $200 million to produce, has become the third-highest-grossing movie of all time, behind two of James Cameron's movies, *Titanic* (1997) and *Avatar* (2009). *The Force Awakens*, directed by J. J. Abrams, also shattered, smashed, and set fire to scores of other records, ending with a total box-office run of more than $2.1 billion.

TRANSPORTATION RECORDS

This collection of the bizarre, impressive, marvelous, and downright silly means of transportation would get some strange looks down Main Street.

Lawn Mower Mover

http://y2u.be/nF18um9VGp8

Next time you complain about mowing your scrubby 10-foot patch of grass, consider investing in a Honda Mean Mower. With a custom-made Cobra sports seat, a six-speed gear system, and a fiberglass cutter deck, Honda claims their machine is the world's fastest mower. It is capable of speeds of up to 130 miles per hour. Piers Ward of BBC's *Top Gear* magazine took the grass-cutting speedster for a spin in Tarragona, Spain, and managed 116.57 miles per hour—it was, indeed, a lawn mower land-speed record!

▼ Fast-Speed John

http://y2u.be/FACWhm_8lmY

When you've got to go, you've got to go—quickly! No one knows that more than plumber Colin Furze, from Lincolnshire, England. Luckily, Colin is also an engineer and an inventor, so he was able to build the world's fastest toilet. With a powerful 140cc motorbike engine hidden under the seat, Furze smashed the previous record of 42.25 mph with his 55 mph lightning lavatory. See Furze's YouTube channel for other record breakers, including a mobility scooter and a baby carriage.

THE WORLD'S FASTEST JOHN

One-Wheel Wonder

http://y2u.be/Jzeq7FWl3Dg

The idea behind the monowheel is simple: Build a big enough wheel and you can fit a person inside. Motorized monowheels have been around since the 1930s, but issues with balance, steering, and visibility make them dangerous to ride. Kevin Scott built his monowheel, *War Horse*, from a 200cc go-kart engine. It has a diameter of 59 inches and the only way to change direction is by leaning. Nevertheless, in September 2016, in Yorkshire, England, Kev rode along an airstrip and back, clocking up a record speed of 61 mph.

◢ Time for Bed

http://y2u.be/CQYWX9UaCjQ

Tom Onslow-Cole is a top British racing driver who specializes in driving souped-up road cars and sports cars. His recent triumph, however, came in bed—a speeding bed. Tom traveled to the Emirates Motorplex dragstrip in the United Arab Emirates to drive a motorized bed, based on a specially modified Ford Mustang. Never one to be caught napping, he hit a top speed of 84 miles per hour. Tom has held a world record before. In 2012, he helped drive the world's fastest milk float. In 2014, that record was broken, but at least he won't lose any sleep over it now.

EARTH'S BEST SPACE EXPLORER

▲ Mars Marathon

https://www.youtube.com/watch?v=EADbiFTHirk

NASA's Opportunity Rover has been roving around the Red Planet for more than ten years, traveling more than 25.9 miles and, in July 2015, the little adventurer 60 million miles from home broke the record for the greatest distance ever traveled on another planet. "Opportunity has driven farther than any other wheeled vehicle on another world," John Callas, part of NASA's Jet Propulsion Laboratory, said of Opportunity's achievements. "This is remarkable considering Opportunity was only intended to drive one kilometer." Keep on going, Opportunity!

BIZARRE PEOPLE

They say: "If you've got it, flaunt it." None of these record breakers seems to have any problem flaunting their special features. And, as you will discover, they are pretty special.

▼ Leg Work

The sports coach at George Mason High in Virginia can regale her pupils with her experiences as a top Russian basketball player. But you suspect they might be more impressed with another area in which she excels. For Svetlana Pankratova has the world's longest female legs. Her pins stretch 4 feet 4 inches, more than two-thirds of her total height of 6 feet 5 inches.

THE WOMAN WITH THE LONGEST LEGS

◀ Tongue-Tied

http://y2u.be/h3Ys5aWrbNc

Byron Schlenker always thought his tongue was a real mouthful, but he never dreamed it could be a record breaker until he helped his 14-year-old daughter, Emily, with a school project. Seeing a picture of an Australian man who claimed to have the world's widest tongue, he began to wonder if his own tongue measured up. Soon he discovered that not only did he have an even wider tongue, but also that Emily had the record female equivalent! Byron's measures a whopping 3.78 inches across—0.75 inch wider than an iPhone 6—and Emily is not far behind at 2.87 inches.

▶ What a Waist

http://y2u.be/zcDlcYQmkdo

Cathie Jung first wore a corset at her wedding in 1969. She and her husband liked the look and now she is the corset queen—wearing the constrictive garment 24 hours a day. Her devotion to corsetry has enabled Cathie to reduce her waist to a record-breaking 15 inches—about the size of a jar of mayonnaise. It is an achievement even more remarkable when you consider her bust and hips are a pretty average 39 inches.

Polydactilistic

https://www.youtube.com/watch?v=Rx05Mo1wWT4

When it comes to fingers and toes, ten of each seems to be enough for most people. For lucky Devendra Suthar of Himatnagar, Gujarat, India, however, being a "normal" person with 20 digits gets a big thumbs down—he has 28 in total! Born with a condition called polydactylism, Devendra, a carpenter (obviously good with his hands!), has 14 fingers and 14 toes and has been awarded the honor of the person with the most number of fingers and toes, after being verified by the Guinness World Records team in December 2015.

105

EXTREME EATING

The world of competitive eating is not for the fainthearted or for those brought up not to shovel down their food. However, it is pretty amazing.

Cone Madness

https://www.youtube.com/watch?v=RfRDA1Tbwko

WORLD'S LARGEST ICE-CREAM CONE

Being surrounded by freezing-cold temperatures, as well as constant snow and ice, you'd think that Norwegians would be sick to their stomachs at the thought of eating chilly ice cream. But not so. Norway's popular ice-cream company, Hennig-Olsen, scooped a Guinness World Records title in July 2015 after creating the world's tallest ice-cream cone ever—a magnificent 10-foot 1-inch feat of deliciousness. Weighing a ton, literally, the cone contained 237.5 gallons of strawberry ice cream—enough for 10,800 people to have two scoops each—and had to be airlifted to the event by helicopter.

The Grape Man

http://y2u.be/BmdoO53-Bol

Steve "The Grape Man" Spalding discovered his skill when his college roommates began throwing candies around the room. Steve amazed his friends by catching everything thrown at him—in his mouth! Over the following 15 years, he practiced and honed his skills and concentrated on catching grapes. He is now the proud possessor of a host of records, including catching 116 in 3 minutes and 1,203 in 30 minutes. It's not clear, however, whether he eats them all.

▶ Sprout About It

https://www.YouTube.com/watch?v=7Jl8gf2V98U

For many people, Brussels sprouts represent the unacceptable side of Christmas dinner, left on the side when all else has been polished off. This is not the case for Emma Dalton. The surprisingly slim 27-year-old competitive eater, who has stuffed back a 5,000-calorie burger in under 10 minutes, has worked her way through the world's biggest helping of sprouts. In one sitting lasting just over half an hour, she scoffed 325 of the mini cabbages—that's almost 7 pounds of festive veggie. However, not even Emma seems to actually like sprouts, because she coated them in mint sauce, gravy, and ketchup to help wash them down.

WORLD RECORD BRUSSELS SPROUTS EATER

▶ Kobayashi— the Master Eater

http://y2u.be/P1GBf0ioYKI

Kobayashi (see page 37) is arguably the world's greatest competitive eater. He has been blowing away his rivals in competitions for 15 years. He has pigged down hot dogs, tacos, satay, noodles, and even cow brains, all in world-record time. Here is the master in action on a TV show in 2012, in which he set the record for most Twinkies eaten in a minute. Eating just one "Golden Sponge Cake with Creamy Filling" can be delightful; however, two Twinkies can be sickly. Kobayashi ate 14.

THE CHAMPION COMPETITIVE EATER

▼ Blowing Bubbles

http://y2u.be/alBUeRNOalw

Champion bubble blower Chad Fell of Alabama blew a bubblegum bubble with a diameter of 20 inches that remained intact for a full 5 seconds. It was no fluke. Chad takes his skill seriously. He gets through two bags of Dubble Bubble a week in practice and knows his science. He drinks cold water to regulate the temperature in his mouth and chews for 15 minutes to cut down the sugar to aid elasticity before carefully adding air.

▼ Oh, Crumbs

http://y2u.be/OZMMSW4Ackk

Many of the records in this book are impossible for readers to try at home. They are either dangerous, expensive, require specific skills, or are just too gross. So here's one you can try yourself. All you need is a chocolate muffin and a camera. Watch the video, study the tactics of Kyle Thomas Moyer of Pennsylvania, who set the record for the fastest time to eat a muffin without using your hands, and prepare your attempt. The target to beat is 28.18 seconds, and remember—no hands!

Egg-ceptional

http://y2u.be/uCgok8lmVoI

Not only does speed-eating heroine Sonya Thomas rank among the best in her field, she also has the best nicknames. She sometimes goes under the fantastic moniker "The Leader of the Four Horsemen of the Esophagus." More often she is known as "The Black Widow" in recognition of the 112-pound petite woman's ability to outeat men four times her size. As well as the feat seen here, Sonya holds other records, not least consuming nearly 5 pounds of fruitcake in 10 minutes.

Furious—and Tearful

http://y2u.be/Jky1gDSw0AM

Furious Pete (real name Pete Czerwinski) is a major player in the competitive eating world. He holds six world records, including polishing off 17 bananas in 2 minutes, wolfing down 15 hamburgers in 10 minutes, and guzzling a bottle of olive oil (25 fluid ounces) in 60 seconds. Pete confesses that eating a whole onion in 43 seconds was the toughest of all. Watch his first failed attempt, and you'll see why.

MuLTIPLE FOOD-EATING WORLD RECORD HOLDER

NICE MOVES!

These entertaining clips pay homage to agile people who have danced themselves into a pirouetting, head-spinning, pole-leaping, tip-tapping, mascot jiving, record-breaking world.

Spinning Queen

http://y2u.be/_bT756ywafU

Since she was ten, Sophia Maria Lucia has been America's darling. The young ballerina appeared on hit TV shows, such as *Dancing with the Stars*, *America's Got Talent,* and *The Ellen DeGeneres Show*. The dance prodigy has her own dancewear line and even a book. There is no denying the girl has talent and now she has a new nickname: "The Spinning Queen." In this clip, filmed in 2013, Sophia performs an amazing world-record 55 consecutive pirouettes.

▼ Body Popping

http://y2u.be/yHzpcBuQlpM

Julia Gunthel goes by the stage name Zlata. A 27-year-old Russian living in Germany, she is also known as the Most Flexible Woman on Earth. Watching the way she twists and bends her body around, it is hard to imagine that Julia actually has a spine. Her balloon-bursting act just has to be seen to be believed. She manages to burst three balloons in 12 seconds, using the curve of her back as a press. That just can't be comfortable.

▶ Human Propeller

https://youtu.be/EZfVAxG2-h4

The headspin, a staple power move of break dancing, is a routine where the dancer's body is rotated while standing on his head. Just watch the poise and strength of 23-year-old Aichi Ono of Japan as it seems he tries to screw his head into the ground. The Human Tornado, or Spinboy as he is also called, spins at a breakneck speed, racking up an incredible 142 rotations in a minute on a TV show in Japan.

RECORD-BREAKING NUMBER OF HEADSPINS

Limbo Queen

https://www.youtube.com/watch?v=tqI4NKLhhvU

Shemika Charles is the world-famous Limbo Queen. Ever since setting fire to the Guinness World Record for doing the limbo a mere 8.5 inches from the floor live on TV in 2010, Charles has traveled the world, showing off her unique talent. In June 2015, however, the Limbo Queen took her skills to a whole new low—and limboed *under a car!* The first world record of its kind and genuinely unbelievable!

Pole Dance

http://y2u.be/k60aeDbB_vw

The Cheraw Dance, which involves dancers stepping in and out between a pair of horizontal bamboo poles, is a skillful and mesmeric folk dance. As part of the Chapchar Kut, a harvest festival in Mizoram in northeast India, more than 11,900 dancers in traditional costumes gathered to perform the dance. Using 6,710 bamboo sticks and dancing on a football field and 1.86 miles of road, they set a new world record as the largest and longest bamboo dance.

THAT'S GOTTA HURT!

"Now that has got to hurt." Sometimes you feel as if you are about to experience the pain yourself as you watch these record breakers undergo self-torture. Of course you aren't. Still, "Ouch!"

Doing His Nut

http://y2u.be/mkgDDCMKXXc

Next Christmas, when you are wrestling with a pair of nutcrackers and a walnut that won't crack, think back to this clip. It is from the Punjab Youth Festival in Lahore, Pakistan, in 2014. Here, martial-arts expert Mohammad Rashid cracks 155 walnuts in only a minute—using his head. This man is deadly with his own nut, leaving just a wake of broken shells as he heads around the table at breakneck speed.

▼ Push-up Star

https://www.youtube.com/watch?v=PdlpfOPCj9I

Superfit fitness fanatic Carlton Williams, a man with very little body fat, has broken his own world record for the most push-ups successfully completed in 60 minutes. The 50-year-old from Wales achieved 2,220 complete push-ups—lowering his body until a 90-degree angle was attained at the elbow *for every single one*—at a gym in Margaret River, Western Australia, in August 2015. "After a while you just get used to the pain," he admitted afterward. Be honest, how many could *you* do in an hour?

▼ The Flame Game

http://y2u.be/cNuwX0hTFKU

When you take a spoonful of soup and realize slightly too late that it's still too hot for you, that soup is around 185°F. If you're unlucky, your tongue will be blistered for a day or two. Now consider Brad Byers, a man nicknamed the "Human Tool Box" (because he can insert tools through his nasal cavities, but that's another story). Brad trumps your hot soup by more than 20 times as he extinguishes a propane blowtorch on his tongue. Incredibly, he's basically licking a 3,630°F flame—what on earth can his tongue be made of?

▶ Beard of Bees

https://www.youtube.com/
watch?v=izDNnfUkTBw

Ruan Liangming, from China, is either fearless, stupid, or he just really loves bees. In January 2016, he smashed his own previous world record by covering his entire body in the beloved buzzing insect in a nail-biting bid to create the ultimate "bee beard." How many bees does it take to achieve this, I hear you wondering. In fact, it's 637,000, including 60 queen bees! Overall, Ruan successfully set a world record for the heaviest mantle (full body coverage) of bees, which weighed approximately the same as another human being lying on top of you, roughly 140 pounds.

MOST TIME
SPENT
COVERED
IN BEES

▲ Heavy Metal

http://y2u.be/Rj7vKStJmtA

A living confusion of tattoo and glistening metal, Elaine Davidson is the world's most-pierced woman. A Brazilian-born nurse living in Edinburgh, Scotland, Elaine has 462 studs and rings (192 on her face), which saw her crowned the world's most-pierced woman in 2000. But Elaine didn't stop there—as of March 2012, she had amassed more than 9,000 piercings. She never removes the rings and studs, which means she carries around an extra 6.6 pounds. But you wouldn't miss her in a crowd!

THE WOMAN WITH THE MOST PIERCINGS

THE MOST EXPENSIVE

You'll be surprised at some of the things that turn up in the "most expensive" basket in the YouTube supermarket. Who would expect a secondhand car or a flashy pair of sneakers?

◀ Flight of Fancy

http://y2u.be/84WIaK3bl_s

If you're taking a flight from New York City to Sydney, Australia, why not travel in style? In fact, why not book a flight on Etihad Airways' Airbus A380? Ask for their luxury suite, "The Residence." At a mere $52,000, it's the world's most expensive flight. The five-star suite comprises an elegantly furnished double bedroom, a lounge with a flat-screen TV, and a shower room, and comes complete with a Savoy Hotel–trained butler to prepare your bed and ensure your comfort. What's that? You're booked in economy? Oh well, maybe you can wangle yourself an upgrade!

THE MOST EXPENSIVE USED CAR

▼ $50 Million for a Used Car?

http://y2u.be/n2j8ElGBzTU

Only 39 of the beautiful 1962–64 Ferrari 250 GTO cars were ever produced. Originally intended to race at Le Mans and similar events, they were soon superseded, and in the 1970s they fetched as little as $10,000. Now only the super-rich can afford them—if they can find one for sale. No one seems sure of how many exist, but currently the 250 holds the record for most expensive sale at auction ($32 million) and most expensive ever ($52 million in a private sale).

◀ Sting in the Tale

http://y2u.be/RCcY0n_7DDs

The list of the most expensive liquids on earth is fascinating: perfume, champagne, and human blood are all predictably on the list; there are some surprises like maple syrup and nasal spray; and no computer user would be surprised to see printer ink near the top at around $8,000 a gallon. Just be thankful, then, that you don't need too much scorpion venom (used in anticancer medicines). Scorpions are difficult and dangerous to obtain and milk (see the video!) and their venom fetches an amazing $40 million a gallon.

Wallet-Melting Ice Cream

http://y2u.be/PpnujjnP1Eg

It looks like a tasty chocolate ice cream—and at $25,000 so it should! The world's most-expensive dessert, Frrrozen Haute Chocolate is available at New York's famous Serendipity 3 restaurant. They need advance notice of two weeks, because this is not just a slushy frozen mix of cocoa and milk. The dessert contains more than 5 grams of 24-carat gold, and the finest ingredients are flown in from around the globe, including a garnish of La Madeline au Truffe, the most expensive chocolate in the world.

◀ A Well-Traveled Angel

http://y2u.be/CT7AXKmSGRg

Watch this video and there is little doubt that Argentina winger Angel Di María has the potential to be among the world's best. He was man of the match in Real Madrid's Champions League triumph in 2014 and he helped his country make the World Cup final in the same year. But, too often, Di María has disappointed, and such unfulfilled potential has made him the world's most-expensive player. Since his career began at Rosario in Argentina, he has been sold to Benfica (€8 million/$10.8 million), Real Madrid (€25 million/$30.7 million), Manchester United (£59.7 million/$100.5 million), and Paris Saint-Germain (€63 million/$67.4 million)—a cumulative total of $209.4 million in transfer fees.

THE MOST-EXPENSIVE SOCCER PLAYER

A LONG WAY DOWN

Some people just have no respect for the laws of gravity. It might have kept sensible folk's feet on the ground for centuries, but not your adrenaline-junkie record breaker.

The Birdman of Norway

http://y2u.be/ER1PGYe9UZA

Is it a bird? Is it an airplane? No. It's Espen Fadnes, the World's Fastest-Flying Human Being. In his flying-squirrel suit, Norwegian Espen routinely leaps off buildings, bridges, mountains, and cliffs—and then flies. Winning a base-jumping competition in 2010, he officially became the fastest-flying human. Just watch as he calmly (although, to be fair, he admits he's completely terrified) steps off a 4,068-foot cliff in Stryn, Norway, and flies through the air at speeds of more than 150 miles per hour.

Jump de Triomphe

http://y2u.be/MLejkyXbJlc

Australian motorcycle stunt rider Robbie Maddison likes a New Year's Eve party; his record-breaking end-of-year stunts have become a tradition for the thrill seeker. Few of them can beat the 2008 effort when the 27-year-old sped his bike off a 35-foot-high ramp to the top of the 96-foot-high replica of the Arc de Triomphe in Las Vegas. Having set the world record for the highest motorcycle jump, he then plunged the 80-foot drop back—breaking his hand in the process.

THE FASTEST BAREHANDED CLIMBER

▼ Look Mom, Just Hands!

http://y2u.be/Wy3SuhEQHVg

Dan Osman was the fastest barehanded speed climber in the world. In this ascent, he climbs Bears Reach, a 400-foot rock face of Lover's Leap in California, in just 4 minutes 25 seconds. He uses no ropes or grips, just gaining hold with his feet and his bare hands. Osman held other mountain-stunt world records, including a freefall rope jump of 1,100 feet at the Leaning Tower in Yosemite, California. Unfortunately, this was also the spot where he met his death after a tragic rope malfunction.

The Sky's No Limit

http://y2u.be/FQSvowsAUkI

Felix Baumgartner may have been the first and most famous skydiver to break the sound barrier, but his 2012 record lasted little more than two years. In 2014, Alan Eustace, a senior vice president at Google, fell from more than 25 miles above New Mexico, smashing Baumgartner's record. In a custom-made pressurized space suit, he jumped from 135,890 feet, reaching a speed of 822 miles per hour. It is claimed his body set off a sonic boom that could be heard by the recovery team on the ground.

THE HIGHEST FREEFALL JUMP RECORD

▲Walking the Walk

http://y2u.be/9W0umbacmzg

In China, Adili Wuxor is known as the "prince of tightrope walking," so his special skill won't be a surprise. The feat itself, however, might impress. The 45-year-old Wuxor breaks his own record by walking a wire that's 5,905 feet long and about 590 feet above the ground across the Yellow River. He pauses at the center for more than half an hour, performing various stunts on the 1.5-inch-thick wire as he waits for his assistant, who started at the other end. He then proceeds to walk over him and continues his epic walk to the end of the wire.

COOL CONSTRUCTIONS

The world of engineering deserves a special mention in the record-breaking hall of fame. The world's greatest tunnels and bridges are spectacular examples of human achievement.

▶ Bridge of Size

http://y2u.be/WP1rZrB9SZI

Opened in 2009, the Sidu River Bridge in Hubei Province of China is the highest bridge in the world. It is a suspension bridge that hangs a vertiginous 1,600 feet above the river gorge. It spans just over 5,000 feet across the river valley; far enough that builders had to use a rocket to string the first pilot line. Some claim it is also the only bridge in the world high enough for a person to reach terminal velocity if they were to jump off.

THE WORLD'S HIGHEST BRIDGE

◀ Light Fantastic

http://y2u.be/9ugUDYcr9hw

The Bund Sightseeing Tunnel is one of Shanghai's top tourist attractions and it's also the world's longest multicolored light tunnel. Taking just 5 minutes to travel the 2,123 feet under the Huang Pu River in Shanghai, passengers travel in automated cars and experience a psychedelic trip from space to the core of the earth and back again. Some find the journey, full of dazzling lights, strange visual effects, and otherworldly voices, "mind-bending," while others have deemed it "tacky." See what you think . . .

▲ Stairway to Heaven

http://y2u.be/T2HHh5ksUvI

High above the breathtaking scenery of China's Zhangjiajie National Forest Park is a white bridge that seems to sit in the clouds. The Zhangjiajie Grand Canyon Glass Bridge is believed to be the world's longest and tallest glass pedestrian bridge. Located in an area that inspired the floating Hallelujah Mountains of James Cameron's movie *Avatar*, the 1,410-foot bridge stands nearly 984 feet above the ground. Glass panels set into its walkway give visitors vertigo-inducing views and photo opportunities of the canyon below. "It creates an experience of being in pure nature while suspended in midair," said the architect, Haim Dotan.

Little Big Town

http://y2u.be/O8TsKEtR8VQ

Welcome to Casey, Illinois, just a three-hour drive south of Chicago. It might have a population of only 3,000, but this little town is onto a big thing. In 2011, local man Jim Bolin made a 56-foot wind chime to draw business to his wife's tea shop. He and other town folk then crafted a golf tee (29.5 feet), wooden shoes (12 feet), a pitchfork (60 feet), a rocking chair (55 feet), a mailbox (33 feet), and pair of knitting needles (13 feet) with a crochet hook (6 feet)—all, of course, world-record size!

THE MOST DANGEROUS TUNNEL

◣ Cliffhanger

http://y2u.be/GzJnOrr5RUE

Located in the Taihang Mountains of China, the Guoliang Tunnel is deemed the world's most dangerous tunnel. In 1972, inhabitants of the village of Guoliang dug a tunnel 3,937 feet long through the rocky cliff. When opened to traffic, it was soon dubbed "the road that does not tolerate any mistakes." A tight squeeze for even one vehicle, it twists and turns past 30 or so "windows," which provide views off the precipice to a tumbling abyss hundreds of feet below.

WILD RECORD BREAKERS

Another scan of the great achievers of the wild world brings forth the slow-motion sloth, the aggressive ant, the supersize squid, and one very woolly sheep.

THE WORLD'S SLOWEST ANIMAL

▼ Beware of the Bull

http://y2u.be/vU_thoOeQw0

The bulldog ant—also called a bull ant or jumper ant—is the hard case of the insect world. The world's most dangerous ant, it is built for fighting. It measures a whopping 0.59–1.4 inches in length, and it has long mandibles and a venomous sting that inflicts death on other insects and great pain to larger creatures. But what gives them the edge is their fearlessness. They don't take kindly to visitors and will take on anything that comes near, even snakes and humans.

▲ Sloth Motion

http://y2u.be/OTp8W251aiQ

The three-toed sloth doesn't do anything in a hurry. It likes to sleep for around 10 hours a day, and it comes down from its tree once a week to do its business and occasionally have a (slow) swim. These are the world's slowest mammals, averaging a distance of only 0.15 mile per hour, with a top speed of 6.5 feet per minute. They are so slow that algae grow on them. They do, however, have a good excuse; their long claws, ideal for tree life, make walking particularly uncomfortable.

▶ Monster Squid

http://y2u.be/xDcsByYGzSE

Armed with giant tentacles, swiveling hooks, and the world's largest eyes, the colossal squid is the largest invertebrate on the planet. Rarely seen and even more rarely caught, they live in the deep, cold waters of Antarctica. The largest of the species to be caught was a squid 30 feet long, caught by a fishing boat off Antarctica in 2007. The 990-pound monster, whose calamari rings would be as thick as car tires, was immediately frozen and transported to New Zealand. This clip shows what happened when it thawed.

THE WORLD'S LARGEST INVERTEBRATE

◀ Woolly Sweater

http://y2u.be/kHu-r4gx2kI

Hikers in Mulligans Flat Woodland Sanctuary outside Canberra, Australia, came across an extraordinary creature. It was the size of a small car and as woolly as a yeti—it was Chris, a lost and very overgrown merino sheep. The world's woolliest sheep was in a bad way and, carrying five times his normal coat, it's doubtful if he would have survived the fierce heat of the Australian summer. However, shorn of almost half his body weight, Chris was found to be in surprisingly good health and he yielded 89 pounds of wool—the equivalent of 30 sweaters.

SPECTACULAR SCIENCE

Making new discoveries and inventions and exploring deeper and farther than ever is the business of the scientist. So it is no surprise that they set some pretty incredible records.

Wonderstuff

http://y2u.be/WFacA6OwCjA

Graphene is a thin layer of pure carbon; it is a single, tightly packed layer of carbon atoms that are bonded together in a hexagonal honeycomb lattice. It is the thinnest, lightest, and toughest material known to man, as well as being the best conductor of heat and electricity. Recent scientific breakthroughs in its production have led to predictions that it will soon be used in everything from bulletproof clothing to fold-up televisions and phones, and even invisibility cloaks.

▼ Bye-Bye Moon

http://y2u.be/uKexFyfhwkg

Only 12 men have even taken a step on the Moon. Just three years after Neil Armstrong's first great step, Eugene Cernan prepared to climb back into *Apollo 17* as the last man on the Moon. While there, Cernan set the land speed record in the Lunar Rover, 11.2 miles per hour, and spent a longer time than anyone else on the lunar surface. "When I pulled up the ladder," he said, "I knew I wasn't going to be coming this way again."

THE LUNAR
SURFACE
LAND SPEED
RECORD

FARTHEST FLIGHT BY HOVERBOARD

▲ Board Game

http://y2u.be/rNKRxsNyOho

They promised us jetpacks but, in the meantime, the hoverboard will suit us just fine. Here's Franky Zapata setting a new world record in April 2016 for the longest hoverboard flight, as he zooms 7,388 feet over the sea off the coast of France and then lands safely back on dry land. The hoverboard is powered by jet-engine propulsion and the direction is controlled by the rider's feet. Wearing a backpack full of fuel, you can fly for around 10 minutes, reaching heights of 10,000 feet and hitting a top speed of 95 miles per hour.

▶ Leading Light

http://y2u.be/3bIXUBXj070

LIGHTEST SOLID MATERIAL IN THE WORLD

Clever Chinese scientists have created the world's lightest solid material—a graphene aerogel that is seven times lighter than air and 12 percent lighter than the previous record holder. The spongelike matter, made of freeze-dried carbon and graphene oxide, is also the thinnest material ever made—a pile of three million graphene sheets stands at just 0.039 inch (1 millimeter) high—but its unique structure also makes it very light and strong. In fact, the claim is that a single sheet as thin as plastic wrap could withstand the weight of an elephant.

UNLIKELY CELEBRITIES

The millions of YouTube viewers can create the most unlikely celebrity record breakers. Among the surprising superachievers are a scooting dog and a bunch of dancing hardened criminals.

▼ Exercise Yard

http://y2u.be/vsG1_eee9fg

The Philippines prisoners' dance to "Thriller" was a YouTube hit and is still worth viewing, but this full-body resistance workout by prison inmates in Peru broke their world record for the most people dancing in a prison. The colorful display was the result of three months' practice by around 1,200 prisoners at the overcrowded Lurigancho prison in Lima. The workout saw the prisoners—many of them murderers, drug barons, and other serious offenders—strutting their stuff to the sounds of the beats of reggaeton and merengue.

▲ Quick Hit

http://y2u.be/0E00Zuayv9Q

"I have a pen. I have an apple. Apple-pen! I have a pen. I have [a] pineapple. Pineapple-pen!" Oh, you mock now but, once you hear it, you'll be singing it all day long. The song "Pineapple-Apple-Pen" by Piko-Taro, a 40-year-old Japanese DJ, tapped perfectly into the winning formula of catchy lyrics, a memorable beat, and a hilariously simple dance routine. His YouTube video has now garnered more than 100 million views, his Facebook video has had 70 million views, and his single—a mere 45 seconds in length—became the shortest song ever to make the Top 100 in the United States.

MOST PRISONERS DANCING EVER

Amazing Afro

http://youtu.be/65-He8_sb_k

Fourteen years ago, inspired by an old photo of her mother sporting an afro hairstyle, Aevin Dugas, from Louisiana, swapped her straight locks for her own natural round style. Now she sports the world's largest natural afro, measuring 4 feet 4 inches around and 7 inches tall. It takes two days to wash and dry her afro and she sometimes struggles to see out from it, but she does admit it makes a really comfortable pillow.

▼ Dog on Wheels

hhttp://y2u.be/qKYryJ_1poQ

He's a three-year-old French sheepdog with a special talent. Ever since he was a puppy, Norman has been climbing on board a scooter and propelling himself along. Norman balances himself on the scooter with his two front paws on the handle and a back paw on the scooter. He uses his other hind paw to push himself forward. Having already earned the moniker "Norman the Scooter Dog," he then scooted about 33 feet in just over 20 seconds—a world record for a dog on a scooter!

A Real Mouthful

http://yt.vu/PampEBRmyzQ

Vijay Kumar of Bangalore, India, is getting used to the words "open wide." It's not just the dentist who wants to peer into the mouth of this world-record holder, for Vijay has 37 teeth in his mouth—five more than the average person and more than anyone else in the world. Vijay first noticed his bite was unusual as a teen, but only when he reached his twenties did he think of checking just how toothy he was. He does complain of biting his tongue but, on the other hand, he never has any trouble chewing caramels!

BEST CANINE ON A SCOOTER

WORLD OF WONDER

Movie star George Clooney famously said, "I go on YouTube when somebody says to look something up." I wonder if he found any of these fabulous clips?

▼ Who You Calling a Dummy?

http://youtu.be/EmkUGEirTE8

If you are the kind of person who gets spooked by ventriloquist dummies, this clip could make you feel a little uneasy. It contains wonderfully creepy footage of the dolls on display at the Vent Haven museum in Kentucky. With more than 800 objects in the museum, they have the largest collection of ventriloquist dolls in the world—from a figure that was fashioned by a World War II German POW to Dolly, a dummy crafted in 2009, complete with diamond sparkling teeth.

▲ Carpet World

http://youtu.be/JeEqpKr1vFg

Each year during the holy week preceding Easter, "sawdust carpets" line the city streets in Guatemala. Made of fine, brightly colored sawdust with dried fruit, flowers, and bread, they create an incredible street art of varying and often intricate design. In Guatemala City in April 2014, the longest-ever sawdust carpet was laid. Using an estimated 54 tons of dyed sawdust , it measured 6,600 feet long—but in a matter of days it was trampled away by religious processions.

THE LARGEST COLLECTION OF DUMMIES

▼ Blast Off . . . and Back!

https://www.youtube.com/watch?v=uSmNid9L4fo

For decades, humans have been sending rockets into space, but they've never returned. With the construction of the Falcon-9 craft, U.S. company SpaceX has for the first time ever, in December 2015, successfully landed an unmanned rocket upright, after it completed the task of delivering 11 satellites into orbit. The Falcon-9 flight, which also went twice as high as any rocket of its type had ever done before, proved that when it comes to reusing rockets, and the future of space tourism and travel, the sky is no longer the limit.

MOST POWERFUL REUSABLE ROCKET

A Lot of Nerf

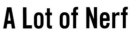

http://y2u.be/57MKxz4pJKE

"Nerf or Nothin'—Accept No Substitutes" runs the slogan for Hasbro's Nerf Blaster toy gun. This, however, is one substitute that's somewhat tempting. Former NASA engineer Mark Rober got together with YouTubers the Eclectical Engineers to construct the world's largest Nerf Gun. The shooter, which looks remarkably like the real thing, is around 5 feet long. Powered by a paintball air tank, it can shoot plastic darts at about 40 miles per hour from a distance of more than 325 feet.

◀ Out of this World

http://yt.vu/E-mR4LCi9nk

A long time ago, in an era far, far away, a special movie spawned a whole array of related merchandising. In 1977, Steve Sansweet was working at the *Wall Street Journal* and came across a promotional book for an upcoming movie called *Star Wars*—it began a lifelong obsession. The movie generated a myriad of associated products and Steve began to collect them. Now housed in a 9,000-square-foot facility an hour north of San Francisco named Rancho Obi-Wan, his display—the biggest *Star Wars* collection in the world—numbers around 90,000 items with another 200,000 or so in storage awaiting classification.

▼ It's All Relative

http://youtu.be/WebTR66FJPc

Sect leader Ziona Chana has 39 wives—all sharing a 100-room mansion in a holy village in India. The largest family in the world lists 32 sons, 18 daughters, 22 grandsons, 26 granddaughters, and 7 great-grandchildren all living under one roof. While the youngest wife gets the bedroom next to Ziona, the eldest wife runs the household and organizes the meals, which can see them preparing 30 chickens, peeling 130 pounds of potatoes, and boiling more than 200 pounds of rice.

THE LARGEST FAMILY IN THE WORLD

PEOPLE POWER

One day in the far-flung future, everyone will hold a record for something. These guys have already made their mark, but there's a record out there for everyone.

Souped-Up Cart

https://youtu.be/HcCoVFhdO3g

This crazy record-breaking invention is guaranteed to make the trip to the grocery store a lot more fun. Rodney Rucker of Arizona has created a V8-power shopping cart 16 feet tall—the largest motorized shopping cart in the world. This fantastic vehicle sits six people comfortably in the basket, with another person behind the wheel in the "child's seat." Although the cart can comfortably cruise along at 60 miles per hour, it's probably best not to do that down the frozen-vegetable aisle.

▼ Hard Core

http://yt.vu/pTeuBq1ai5g

They say an apple a day keeps the doctor away, but probably not the way Johnny Strange deals with them. The British daredevil, bored with breaking the record for the heaviest weight lifted by pierced ears (33 pounds), looked for something even more impressive. So he took to chopping apples with a chainsaw—while holding them in his mouth. Johnny claims he's never had any accidents, but that's not simply good fortune. He puts it down to meticulous practice, explaining that it normally takes about two years to bring a trick to the stage.

▶ Hot to Trot

https://youtu.be/8o_pNN3Ndy0

The feat of firewalking, treading barefooted over burning ashes, has been explained scientifically. Put simply, the amount of time the foot is in contact with the hot surface is minimized in order to prevent the soles of the feet from burning. However, it's not everyone's idea of fun, and many still come away from the activity with burns to their feet. Master firewalker Scott Bell braved temperatures of up to 1,300°F as he trod a record 328 feet over burning coals—then walked away unharmed.

▶ Heads Up, Bro!

https://www.YouTube.com/watch?v=lq_HaPrRmJM

Fans of TV's *Game of Thrones* might recognize the setting for this record as the Great Sept of Baelor. It is, in fact, the Cathedral of Girona in Spain, where Vietnamese circus artists Giang Quoc Co and Giang Quoc Nghiep chose to perform their amazing world-record head-to-head balancing act. The acrobats climbed 90 of the picturesque steps of the cathedral in one minute with one brother balanced on top of the other, using only head-to-head contact. It wasn't the time for the brothers to fall out and, fortunately, they kept clear heads and held any sibling rivalry in check.

WORLD'S BEST BALANCERS

▶ High Kicking

https://www.YouTube.com/watch?v=VE9oUefYjqs

Twenty-three-year-old Canadian Silvana Shamuon is no novelty act. Silvana has been practicing martial arts for more than 17 years. She received her junior black belt at the age of 11, was inducted into the Universal Black Belt Hall of Fame in 2007, and represents her country in international tournaments. So, for some fun, Silvana attempted the world record for the most items kicked off people's heads in one minute. Students from her old high school lined up wearing football helmets fitted with golf tees and footballs. Needing to beat 67 for the record, Silvana wound up her powerful kicking leg . . .

▼ Bearded Woman

http://y2u.be/rgQjfcpG7XY

After enduring years of bullying, 25-year-old Harnaam Kaur turned herself into a body-confidence advocate, model, and Instagram star. The brave story of the youngest woman to have a full beard is an inspiring one. Diagnosed with polycystic ovaries, Harnaam has had facial hair since the age of 12. She experienced abuse and threats but, at the age of 15, she decided to stop hiding and confront gender stereotypes. She never looked back. As she told the British *Guardian* newspaper, "They can try to make a freak show out of me, but my voice and my message [are] much stronger than that. I have power in my voice."

RECORD-BREAKING ROBOTS

Science fiction doesn't seem to stay in the movies and books for very long these days. Robots, laser guns, supermaterials, even robo-bees, are already in the record books.

Drone Delivery

http://y2u.be/vNySOrI2Ny8

In recent years, drones are being increasingly used for everyday functions. With technology becoming cheaper and drones stepping into our lives in almost every way, it was only a matter of time before Amazon sent their first *extra* special delivery. In December 2016, Amazon sent the first drone package using Prime Air to Richard B. in Cambridge, England. Taking only 13 minutes to arrive from the moment it was ordered, this was an impressive display from the Internet giant. Richard B. looked pretty pleased with the service at least!

▼ Eye in the Sky

https://www.youtube.com/watch?v=u-vxo_yMQwk

Up, down, left, right . . . No matter where you look these days, drones are never far away. They have become our eyes in the skies. In November 2015, Intel Corporation lit up the skies above the Flugplatz Ahrenlohe in Tornesch, near Hamburg, Germany, with 100 small drones flying in fantastic formation. A year later, in November 2016, they went one better—or 400 to be precise—with 500 drones all controlled by one pilot. Acting as one, they created a stunning Technicolor light show as dazzling as any fireworks display. It's unbelievable, and earned Intel a Guinness World Record for most unmanned aerial vehicles.

LARGEST DRONE DISPLAY

▼ Metal!!!

https://youtu.be/3RBSkq-_St8

We've gotten used to seeing weird-looking rock bands, but this is something else. They are called Compressorhead and they play rock covers, including songs by the Ramones and Nirvana. Compressorhead comprises four-armed Stickboy on drums and 79-digited Fingers on guitar, while Bones plays bass. They are all built from scrap metal and they are the world's first robot rock band. They rock as hard as any band, are better behaved (when turned off), and they don't demand drugs and alcohol— just an electric outlet and a little oil.

THE WORLD'S FIRST ROBOT BAND

Robo-Record

https://www.youtube.com/watch?v=by1yz7Toick

If you ever wanted proof that artificial intelligence is getting closer to taking over the world, then take a peek at the incredible footage that emerged in January 2016 of the fastest robot to ever solve a Rubik's Cube. It's astonishing! Designed by engineer Albert Beer, from Germany, the smart machine, named Sub 1, solved the famously difficult puzzle in just 0.887 seconds! How did it do it? Watch the video to find out.

FASTEST ROBOT TO SOLVE RUBIK'S CUBE

SEEING IS BELIEVING

How often do you hear or read of a record and think, "Surely that's just not possible." If only you could see for yourself . . .

Miniature Machine

http://y2u.be/cSg-yFZ7y0A

In the UK it's called a Heath Robinson contraption, while in the United States they call it a Rube Goldberg machine. In France it's an *usine à gaz* (gas refinery), but the Germans are closest in describing it, calling it a *Was-passiert-dann-Maschine* (what-happens-next machine). This video features the smallest ever of these complex devices. Made with incredible precision for an ad for Japanese watch company Seiko, this intricate and beautiful machine uses 1,200 mechanical watch parts, some of which are smaller than a millimeter in size. In action, it's mesmerizing and somewhat magical.

RECORD-BREAKING ROCKERS

◀ Rock Record

http://y2u.be/EFEmTsfFL5A

Having No. 1 albums around the world just isn't enough for some bands. In the video for their single "Ain't It Fun," American rock band Paramore set 10 world records, including: fastest time to smash 30 clocks with guitars (31.33 seconds); most feathers caught in 30 seconds (18); most vinyl records broken in one minute (58); fastest time to run backward for 30 feet while holding stuffed animals and wearing a blindfold (6.14 seconds); and, of course, most world records set in a music video (10).

▶ Fatal Frog

http://y2u.be/sfENSyycPQ4

They may be just 1–2 inches long, but certain species of the poison dart frog are the most toxic animals in the world. These brightly colored amphibians are found in the rain forests of Central and South America. Their name comes from the practice of some tribes of lacing their blowgun arrows with the poison that coats the frog's skin. The golden poison dart frog, for example, contains enough poison to kill ten adult men.

▼ Flying Bum

http://y2u.be/CWiRZXW8t5I

Just why they call it the "Flying Bum" you can judge for yourself. The *Airlander 10*, part plane and part airship, is the world's largest aircraft. It's enormous at 302 feet long—about 50 feet longer than the biggest passenger jets—with a cargo capacity of 11 tons. The aircraft is eco-friendly, silent, capable of a speed of 90 mph, and is able to land on practically any terrain. It can remain airborne for up to five days on manned flights, but can also float, unmanned, for weeks at a time.

On the Ball

http://y2u.be/GXsacavxteM

There doesn't have to be a point! That's the mantra of Great Ball Contraption (GBC) enthusiasts. A GBC is a machine that receives balls from one module and passes them to another module, like a bucket brigade (or the final contraption in the game Mousetrap). In a hotly contested competition, Maico Arts and Ben Jonkman won back their record for the world's largest Lego GBC with a madcap system of a hundred interconnected lifts, slides, and chutes. To give you an idea of how complex the contraption course is, it takes the ball 16 minutes 30 seconds to travel from start to finish.

COOL CAR STUNTS

Car stunts are some of the most exciting clips on the site. These drivers risk life and limb to perform incredible record-breaking tricks and skills on four wheels.

▶ Wheelie Something

http://y2u.be/ggVpCOT9ZqY

Pulling a side-wheelie (driving on just one front and back wheel) in a car is a technically difficult and ludicrously dangerous feat. To drive along on two wheels at breakneck speed is taking it to another level. The speed record on two wheels was last set in 1997, so hats off to Finnish stunt driver Vesa Kivimäki, who finally broke the record in October 2016. Driving a BMW 330 fitted with tires specially developed by sponsor Nokian, Kivimäki clocked 115.74 mph in his record-breaking jaunt along the runway at Seinajoki Airport in the southwest of Finland.

▶ Completely Loopy

http://youtu.be/jVS4ts1A-ao

Remember the model cars that looped-the-loop on orange tracks on your living room carpet? Now the Hot Wheels toy manufacturers have taken to performing their stunts in real cars. At the 2012 X Games, Tanner Foust and Greg Tracy raced through a loop 60 feet tall on a death-defying life-size version of the Hot Wheels orange track. Foust, a stuntman in movies such as *Fast and Furious: Tokyo Drift* and *Iron Man 2*, said he had to desperately fight blacking out as he experienced around 7Gs of G-force during the stunt.

TWO-CAR WORLD-RECORD LOOP

Tired Out

http://y2u.be/38hlxUuzx2oJ

The Australians love a burnout—where the brakes keep a vehicle stationary while spinning its wheels, causing the tires to heat up and smoke due to friction. Burnout competitions thrive in Australia, where drivers use modified cars with no rear brakes. At the Summernats car festival in Canberra, billed as Australia's biggest horsepower party, 69 cars took part in the world-record attempt for a simultaneous 30-second burnout. Dozens of expensive tires were shredded, and some even ignited into small rubber fires, as the entire area filled up with clouds of smoke.

▼ Monster Monster

http://youtu.be/-HtZjUwPiJw

At 11,500 pounds in weight, 10 feet 6 inches tall, and riding on 66-inch tires, the legendary monster truck they call Bigfoot was attempting to take back its world long-distance jump record. Bigfoot was the original and most famous monster truck, but had not owned the record for 11 years. It was a matter of pride. Finally, in 2012, after a yearlong modification, Bigfoot 18 was ready. Driver Dan Runte hit the ramp at 80 mph and took off . . .

THE LONG-DISTANCE JUMP RECORD

▼ Ramping It Up

http://youtu.be/L5N7R9Wbe_E

This is the closest you will ever come to seeing a flying car. It was New Year's Eve in Long Beach, California, in 2009, and 20,000 people had come out to see all-action driver Travis Pastrana try something really crazy. Pastrana, a rally champion turned stunt driver, launched his Subaru Impreza STI rally car off a ramp on the Pine Avenue Pier at 91 mph. He soared over Rainbow Harbor before successfully landing on a floating barge 269 feet away—almost 100 feet more than the former jump record.

SMASHING
THE JUMP
RECORD

PET RECORDS

These cool creatures have been officially verified as the biggest, smallest, smartest, and most agile.

▶ Monster Bunny

http://y2u.be/SbADYnhHtGg

Darius the rabbit weighs in at 49 pounds and is the size of a small child. He's the biggest rabbit in the world, but Darius is no freak. His breed, the giant continental, produces large creatures and his mother Alice held the record before him. Five-year-old Darius stretches out to an amazing 4 feet 4 inches long and munches through 4,000 carrots, 120 cabbages, and 730 dog bowls of rabbit mix over the year.

THE WORLD'S BIGGEST RABBIT

Who's a Smart Girl Then?

http://y2u.be/unO5whIUF-M

YouTube is full of videos of dogs, and sometimes cats, performing stunts—but Kili the Senegal parrot can match them trick for trick. She claims an unofficial world record by pulling off 20 tricks in just under two minutes. Her feats begin with the customary parrot skills, such as rope climbing and nodding. Nothing remarkable so far, but carry on watching and you'll see Kili go bowling, match rings to pegs, and perform a basketball slam dunk. Worthy of the record books?

◢ Top Cat

https://www.youtube.com/watch?v=S_Hbbg3awjM

Creme Puff was the world's oldest cat to have ever lived. In human years, Creme Puff made it to the respectable age of 38 years old. When you translate that into cat years, however, this whisker-wise kitty lived to the grand old age of 172! Born in 1967, Creme Puff lived her happy life in Austin, Texas, with loving owner Jake Perry, an expert in feline longevity.

WORLD'S OLDEST CAT

Dog's Chance

http://y2u.be/68PMF7Xxppl

Alex Rothacker, a professional dog handler from Illinois, takes in dogs that are often on the verge of being put down due to their aggression. Sweet Pea, an Australian shepherd/ border collie mix, was one such dog who thrived under Alex's program. Sweet Pea holds a somewhat strange record—the most steps walked down backward by a dog while balancing a 5-ounce glass of water on its head. She achieved ten and here she even does it blindfolded! Sweet Pea became a celebrity in Germany after appearing on a prime-time TV show, but died a few years ago at the age of 19.

▶ My Little Pony

http://y2u.be/6XQtd9cTGFM

Here's another Einstein. Smaller than most human babies, he was just 14 inches high at birth and weighed only 6 pounds. Now completely grown, Einstein stands 20 inches high and is officially the world's smallest stallion. The smallest horse, Thumbalina, is slightly shorter but, unlike her, Einstein is not a dwarf, he is just a mini miniature horse. He does, however, have a big personality. He has his own Facebook page, has appeared on *Oprah,* and even had a book written about him.

THE WORLD'S SMALLEST STALLION

143

AMAZING WEATHER

More meteorological marvels, including the coldest and rainiest places on the earth, the man who was struck by lightning seven times, almighty sandstorms, and the great Chinese floods of 1931.

Pat Packs a Punch

https://www.YouTube.com/watch?v=FiswK5Hja5U

In October 2015, Hurricane Patricia became the strongest storm ever measured on the planet. It developed so fast that, over the course of a day, its category changed from a run-of-the-mill tropical storm to a potentially catastrophic hurricane. Patricia's winds peaked at 202 mph—slightly more powerful than those of Super Typhoon Haiyan, which left more than 7,000 dead in the Philippines in 2013. Thousands were evacuated from the Pacific coast of southwestern Mexico, where the storm was heading but, thankfully, by the time Patricia made land, its ferocity had dropped, merely producing tree-bending winds, torrential rain, flash flooding, and huge waves.

RESTAURANT MARISC FIESTA LOS TIBURONI

Have You Got Your Vest On?

http://y2u.be/-io4gG6k61c

This two-and-a-half-minute rundown of the five places you might need to wrap up warmly visits the globe's extremes: from Arctic points in Canada, Greenland, and Russia to Oymyakon in Siberia, the world's coldest inhabited spot. Pride of place, however, goes to a Russian research station on the ice plateau of central Antarctica. The Vostok station recorded a temperature of −128°F in 1983—still the official record—but in August 2010, a satellite detected nearby pockets of trapped air that dipped as low as −135°F.

◀ Sand-Blasted

Iran has the most sandstorms in the world, as winds gust over its open landscape of dry plateaus, deserts, and salt flats. In 2014, the most-devastating sandstorm hit Iran's capital, Tehran, killing five people, injuring 30, and bringing chaos to the city. As the freak dust storm rolled through the city, giant clouds of sand and dust clogged the air, plunging the streets into darkness. The storm produced winds that reached about 75 mph.

THE WORLD'S WORST SANDSTORM

▼ The Greatest Natural Disaster

https://www.youtube.com/watch?v=392J5y3y_XE

The floods that hit the Republic of China in 1931 make up the deadliest natural disaster ever. A combination of thawing heavy snow, torrential rains, and consecutive cyclones caused the Yangtze River to burst its banks. As the rains continued, the country's other major rivers, the Yellow and the Huai, also flooded. When the waters receded, the damage was estimated to have affected more than 28 million people, and the death toll was around 4 million.

Lightning Never Strikes Twice?

https://www.youtube.com/watch?v=yBfrnYlC8yE

The only man in the world to be struck by lightning seven times was Roy C. Sullivan, a park ranger in the Shenandoah National Park in Virginia. Known as "the human lightning conductor," Roy recovered from every one of these strikes, although he did lose a big toenail, his eyebrows, and his hair and experienced many burns. This ad pokes some fun at his expense but is basically a pretty accurate portrayal of the story of his strikes.

SPORTS HEROES

From the sublime skills of Cristiano Ronaldo to the stars of quirky sports such as bog snorkeling, triathlon juggling, and unicycle trampolining, these people are all record heroes.

Unicycle Trampoline Backflips

http://y2u.be/-XRcXqKu7OI

Canadian Cameron Fraser refers to himself as a contemporary circus artist, and after performing feats like this he can call himself whatever he chooses! No one has come near to his achievement of making consecutive backflips while sitting on a unicycle on a trampoline. Cameron manages three complete flips of 360 degrees despite being perched on a unicycle 3 feet tall. The feat itself appears around 2 minutes 10 seconds into this video full of other pretty cool trampolining exploits.

▼ Ronaldo's Records

http://y2u.be/_blH0bMV0Ww

As well as being the only Spanish League player to score 40 goals in successive seasons, Real Madrid's Cristiano Ronaldo is the player who has scored the highest number of hat tricks in a single season and has scored in every minute of a game. He is the only player to have won all the major trophies at two different clubs; and, earning a salary of more than €20 million ($24 million) per year, he is one of the highest-paid soccer players in the world.

▼ Ouch!

http://y2u.be/3Sa_3SKiz94

Dr. Mak Yuree from Bangladesh is a world-renowned expert in martial arts and an international authority on meditation and mind training. He is probably better known as the man who breaks baseball bats with his tibia. Yuree set a world record shattering three of them in one go, and has since performed the feat on a number of occasions. Sometimes called Thundershin Man, Yuree says he trained for nearly 20 years by kicking tree trunks.

▼ Muddy the Waters

http://y2u.be/UoRXZOQBsSQ

The World Bog Snorkeling Championship, first held in 1985, takes place every August at the dense Waen Rhydd peat bog, near Llanwrtyd Wells in Wales. Bog snorkeling requires competitors to complete two consecutive 60-yard lengths of a water-filled trench cut through a peat bog. Competitors must wear snorkels and flippers, and they must complete the course without using conventional swimming strokes, relying on flipper power alone. Andrew Holmes is the record holder with a time of 84 seconds.

Triathlon Juggling

http://y2u.be/1QoqenZytO8

World-record-adjudication website Record Setter awarded Joe Salter the Weirdest Record of the Year award in 2012. Salter swam 0.25 mile while juggling three balls, then he cycled 16.2 miles while juggling two balls in one hand, and also ran 4 miles while juggling. More incredible still, he managed to do it all in only 1 hour 57 minutes. During the event, he threw his balls nearly 20,000 times and managed not to drop a single one while running or on his bike and dropped just three during the swim.

▼ Cheese Chase

http://y2u.be/xHE3wsQ7Wy0

The Coopers Hill annual event in England is the oldest cheese-rolling competition in the world. A 9-pound Double Gloucester cheese is chased down the hill. The first person to catch it is the winner. However, because the cheese has a one-second start and reaches speeds of 70 miles per hour, this is usually just a race for the finish. Stephen Gyde is the most successful competitor ever with 21 cheeses, and the only competitor to have won all three cheeses in a single year.

CHEESE-ROLLING RECORDS

COOL SPORTS RECORDS

From frantic four-legged running to ninja-powered high kicking, the quest for sporting perfection never ends—and with it comes the sound of clattering records.

Lamps Lights Up League

https://www.youtube.com/watch?v=BsmYcoD6rEo

When it comes to legends of English soccer, you don't get more legendary than Frank Lampard, Chelsea's all-time record goal scorer. But that's not the midfielder's only achievement of note: of the 46 clubs in the English Premier League, Lamps has scored against 39 of them—an official world record—while playing for West Ham United, Chelsea, and Manchester City, between 1995 and 2015.

FOUR-LEGGED-SPRINT RECORD HOLDER

▶ Four Legs Good

http://y2u.be/A3rcWarJOe0

Kenici Ito, a 29-year-old man from Tokyo, Japan, spent more than eight years perfecting a four-legged running style based on the wiry patas monkey of Africa. Neighbors would see him walking around on all fours, and he was even shot at by mistake by hunters when training in the mountains. It all paid off in 2012, when Ito incredibly ran 100 meters in less than 20 seconds. He now runs in four-legged races, but he admits he is still beaten by a fast dog.

Exclusive Club

http://y2u.be/RTAHY6oBtjQ

In one of the most intriguing battles of the record world, Michael Furrh won back his longest golf-club title from multiple record holder Ashrita Furman. On the final swing of the day at Waterchase Golf Club in Fort Worth, Texas, Furrh retook the record for a shot with the longest usable golf club after mastering the technique of using a club measuring 28 feet 1 inch. He successfully hit his ball 59 yards—more than some of us manage with a standard club.

▲ High Kicking

http://y2u.be/Q8c2-YoLrSs

Taekwondo is a martial-art combat and defense discipline that particularly rewards jumping and spinning kicks. The video shows the 23-year-old Colombian fighter Yair Medina setting the world record for a high kick in 2011. His incredible feat requires not only that his foot should reach a height of 9 feet 6 inches—but also that he should have the power to deliver a sharp enough kick to burst a plastic plate secured at that position.

Sam's Ace

http://y2u.be/uqmy9oxEJig

Australian Sam Groth is an accomplished professional tennis player. Although never making his mark in the Grand Slam tournaments, Sam has built a reputation as one of the biggest servers in the game. Playing Uladzimir Ignatik in the 2012 Busan Open Challenger in South Korea, Groth sent down a serve at 163.4 miles per hour, smashing the record of 156 miles per hour set by Ivo Karlovic. After his defeat to Ignatik, Groth noted that, unfortunately, hitting the fastest serve doesn't mean you win the match.

WHAT A RECORD!

If humans were meant to fly, we'd have been born with wings . . . but that's why we have skateboards, in-line skates, ramps, and long bungee elastic!

The Only Way Is Down

http://y2u.be/JXyQ3N4S5oc

Marc Sluszny is the most extreme adventurer in the world. He's set a world record in bungee jumping, dived with a great white shark, and represented Belgium in tennis, fencing, yachting, and bobsledding. In 2012, Marc found a new hobby—running down a building. Here, he is completing a vertical run down the side of the Belgacom tower in Brussels. The tower is 335 feet high and he sprinted down the outside of it in a time of 15.5 seconds—a new world record.

▼ Hairpin Highway Dash

https://www.YouTube.com/watch?v=j7hrJzjKEys

Tongtian Road's nickname is "Heaven-Linking Avenue." It takes visitors to the "Gateway to Heaven"—a natural cave on the side of the Tianmen Mountain in China—but the name also hints at the perils of one of the world's most dangerous roads. Twisting alongside sheer drops, the 6.8-mile road zigzags through 99 sharp turns, rising from 656 feet to 4,265 feet above sea level. In a specially modified Ferrari, racing driver Fabio Barone Mihaela set a record when he sped along the treacherous route in just 10 minutes 31 seconds.

▶ The "1080"

http://y2u.be/tbjzZHuGTng

In March 2012, at the age of 12, Tom Schaar became a skateboarding legend. Less than a year after becoming the youngest skateboarder (and only the eighth ever) to successfully land a "900" (2.5 revolutions in the air), he landed a three-revolution "1080." He was the first skateboarder to successfully attempt the feat despite many efforts from leading boarders. Tom, who expected to spend all day trying to complete the move, was able to nail it on only his fifth attempt.

THE WORLD'S FIRST "1080"

▲ Big Rush

http://y2u.be/FrY6OJk-z0I

The Moses Mabhida Stadium in Durban, South Africa, was built for the FIFA World Cup in 2010. The imposing 54,000-seat venue, instantly recognizable from its beautiful white arches, now hosts sports matches, events, and the world's only stadium swing—the biggest swing of any kind. Those venturing to the top of the stadium are afforded a fabulous 360-degree view of Durban and a chance to ride the Big Rush Adrenaline Swing. This thrilling experience begins with a 196-foot freefall followed by a massive 721-foot arc that takes the rider into the center of the stadium. It is not for the fainthearted!

WORLD'S BIGGEST SWING

▲ Slip 'N' Slide

https://www.youtube.com/watch?v=mA8j0Vaj93Q

There is no greater feeling than making a splash on a waterslide, so imagine the sensation you must feel at the end of the world's longest slip and slide—officially measured at 2,006 feet 10 inches in October 2015—in Amman, Jordan. That's about the same size as seven football fields! Lucky sliders who went for a ride on the slide with their rubber rings took several minutes to slide from start to finish.

WORLD'S LONGEST SLIP AND SLIDE

Scraping the Barrels

http://y2u.be/Q0qRNiUbdkk

Risking life and limb in ludicrous competition is nothing new. Barrel jumping—vaulting barrels on ice skates—appears to have gone out of fashion among the adrenaline fanatics despite having the athleticism, skill and obvious danger of broken bones found in modern extreme sports. So we go back to archive footage from the mid-1960s to see Kenneth Lebel clear a then world record of 16 barrels. He actually went on to set the record at 17, but no footage exists of that jump.

HAIR-RAISING RECORDS

There are some special people for whom "doing their hair" doesn't mean a few minutes with a brush and a mirror. Hairstyles, beards, moustaches, and other follicular follies are their step to stardom.

▶ Bearded Lady

http://y2u.be/pn94aT8wsDk

Vivian Wheeler was born with both male and female body parts, so doctors operated to allow for her to live life as a woman. However, she still has a condition known as hypertrichosis, or wolf syndrome, in which excessive hair grows on the face. At the age of seven she began shaving, and soon she was touring as a circus sideshow. Now at 64 years old and living in Bakersfield, California, Vivian is the proud owner of the longest female beard—reaching to a majestic 11 inches.

THE WORLD'S HAIRIEST WOMAN

◀ Blow-Dry Bunny

http://y2u.be/iUZgEFRoIX8

English Angora rabbits are the supermodels of the rabbit world, regularly sweeping up the prizes at shows. Looking like a basketball-size cotton ball, they're incredibly cute and are the only rabbit that has hair covering their eyes. Prize-winning Angora breeder Betty Chu has 50 of them, and not only does she take them to competitions, but she uses their wool to knit hats, scarves, and mittens. The most famous of them is Francesca, whose sumptuous fur won her the accolade of the rabbit with the longest hair in the world—her coat measured in at 14.37 inches.

THE WORLD'S LONGEST MOHAWK

▼ Hard to Handlebar

http://y2u.be/PKzBzDY5I50

Ram Singh Chauhan of India is the proud owner of the world's longest moustache, stretching an incredible 14 feet. Now 57 years old, he started growing his moustache in 1970. It isn't an easy life—Chauhan spends an hour every day cleaning and combing his moustache, and when it is not on proud display, he has to neatly wrap it around his neck. However, it has brought him prestige and some fame, with appearances in Bollywood movies and the 1983 James Bond movie *Octopussy*.

▲ Tallest Mohawk

http://y2u.be/X__XIPhgH34

Usually, Kazuhiro Watanabe's hair is clipped up so it doesn't drag around his knees. It has taken the Japanese fashion designer 15 years to grow it that long, but it is all part of his record-breaking plan. When Kazuhiro gets dressed up (usually for an outdoor event), he and his stylists go to work with three cans of hair spray and an entire bottle of hair gel. Just three hours later, he has the world's highest mohawk—a spike that is a massive 3 feet 8.6 inches high.

THE LONGEST MOUSTACHE IN THE WORLD

155

Even in our wildest dreams, we can't hope to emulate the feats of some of the record breakers in this book. The achievements of Usain Bolt or Paul McCartney are the result of a talent and dedication possessed by few. Others are born to be record breakers by dint of an exceptional physical attribute—a long tongue, big feet— whether they like it or not! Still, the budding record breaker need not despair. There are plenty of videos in this book to inspire anyone to write their name in the history books.

Perhaps you already have a unique skill or hobby that can rival the record holders. For example, you might have a great talent for jumping or licking your nose or you might have quick reflexes or a steady hand. Your particular skill probably isn't yet at the level of the current record holders; most of the achievements in the book are due to practice and hard work. Start working at it now, however, and who knows what heights you will reach?

You don't have to possess a great physical skill to enter the record books. There are plenty of other entries that are equally impressive. Mental agility is a popular area and there are incredible feats of reading, mathematics, and memory; world-beating collections—of anything from TV-show memorabilia to cereal boxes—form a fascinating aspect of record breaking; and someone needs to organize the large-scale gatherings that beat records.

If you need to research your goal, go online and check the existing record. Some in this book did just that and discovered it was a target they could aspire to and eventually beat. There are various organizations, including sporting bodies, who keep their own statistics. Most famously, the *Guinness Book of Records* (www.guinnessworldrecords.com) has been keeping records since 1955 and has a comprehensive database and an online application process.

If you are looking to set a more unusual record, it might be worth consulting recordsetter.com, where you will find inspiration and challenges for all kinds of records—many of which can be attempted in your own kitchen or bedroom. If you care for taking on other people's records, you can always invent your own category. You'll definitely have a record, but don't count on keeping it for long—it's a mighty competitive record-breaking world.

INDEX

CREDITS

The publishers would like to thank the following sources for their kind permission to reproduce the photographs in this book.

4 AFP Photo/Vano Shlamov/Getty Images, 5 Peter Parks/AFP/Getty Images, 7 Geoffrey Robinson/REX/Shutterstock, 8 (bottom) Professor Splash/Barcroft USA/Getty Images, (top) Felipe Caicedo/AFP/Getty Images, 9 Fotodive.ch/Wilfried Niedermayr, 10 (left) Arkaprava Ghosh/Barcroft India, 10 (right) Courtesy of William Winram, 11 Raymond Boyd/Getty Images, 12 (left) Moviestore/REX/Shutterstock, 12 Imaginechina/REX/Shutterstock, 13 Sascha Steinbach/Getty Images, 14 (top) Boris Shevchuk/Shutterstock, 14 Claudia Naerdemann/Shutterstock, 15 (top) Hagen Hopkins/Getty Images, (bottom) Matt Cardy/Getty Images, 16. Shaun Botterill/Getty Images, 17. (top) Richard Bord/Getty Images, (bottom) Cameron Spencer/Getty Images, 18 Stan Honda/AFP/Getty Images, 19 (top) Shutterstock, (bottom) Universal History Archive/UIG via Getty Images, 20 (top) Shutterstock, (bottom) Mark Moffett/Minden Pictures/Getty Images, 21–23 Shuterstock, 24 Bettmann/Getty, 25 (top) AFP Photo/Vano Shlamov/Getty Images (bottom) Drew Simon/AP/Press Association Images, 26 EPA/Rungroj Yongrit, 27 Shutterstock.com, 28 Shutterstock.com, 29 (top) Julian Finney/Getty Images, (bottom) Shutterstock.com, 30 (top) Gregory Varnum via Wikimedia Commons, (bottom) Dusso Janladde, (bottom) Ernesto, 31 TowersStreet, 32–33 Shutterstock.com, 34 Fred Duval/FilmMagic/Getty Images, 35–36 Shutterstock.com, 37 (top) Nils Jorgensen/REX/Shutterstock, (bottom) Shutterstock.com, 38 Oli Scarff/Getty Images, 39. Mario Tama/Getty Images, 40 (top) Shutterstock.com, (bottom) ZUMA Press, Inc/Alamy, 41 (top) Ronaldo Schemidt/AFP/Getty Images, (bottom) Ray Tang/REX/Shutterstock, 42–43 Shutterstock.com, 44 Mark Rolston/AFP/Getty Images, 45 (top) Thomas Senf/Red Bull News Ro/Sipa/REX/Shutterstock, (bottom) Photo by Rauke Schalken with Leica, 46–47 Carl Court/AFP/Getty Images, 48 (left) Shutterstock.com, (right) Moviestore Collection/REX/Shutterstock, 49 (top) Angus Murray /Sports Illustrated/Getty Images, (bottom) Michael Regan/Getty Images, 50–51 Ray Tang/REX/Shutterstock, 52–53 USN Collection/Alamy, 54 (top) Shutterstock.com, (bottom) John Robertson/Barcroft Cars/Barcroft Media via Getty Images, 55 (top) Angela Weiss/Getty Images, (bottom) Shutterstock.com, 56–57 Shutterstock.com, 58 Dan Callister/REX/Shutterstock, 59 (top) DFree/Shutterstock (bottom) Ian MacNicol/Getty Images, 60 East News/REX/Shutterstock, 61 (top) Zhukov Oleg/Shutterstock, (bottom) Tim Matsui/Getty Images, 62–63 Shutterstock, 64 Shutterstock, 64–65 Moviestore Collection/REX/Shutterstock, 65 Shutterstock, 66 (top) Michael Bowles/REX, (bottom) John Springer Collection/Getty Images, 67 ScoKevin Mazur/WireImage/Getty Images, 68 Shutterstock.com, 69 (top) Shutterstock.com, (bottom) Getty Images, 70 Shutterstock, 71 (top) AFP Photo/Gent Shkullaku/Getty Images, (bottom) Obuda University, 72 (top) Shutterstock.com, (bottom) Dimore/Shutterstock, 73 (top) AFP Photo/Vano Shlamov/Getty Images, (bottom) Victor Fraile/Getty Images, 74 (top) Geoffrey Robinson/REX/Shutterstock (bottom) Shutterstock.com, 75 AFP Photo/Ben Stansall/Getty Images, 76 Julien Warnand/epa, 77 (top) Shutterstock.com, (bottom) Yuriy Dyachyshyn/AFP/Getty Images, 78 Shutterstock.com, 79 (top) Laurentiu Garofeanu/Barcroft USA/Barcroft Media via Getty Images, (bottom) Splash News, 80 Dave Mangels/Getty Images for Sony, 81 (top) The Siberian Times, (bottom) PTI (Press Trust of India), 82–83 Piti A Sahakorn/LightRocket via Getty Images, 84 (top) Josh Edelson/AFP/Getty Images, (bottom) Shutterstock.com, 85 (top) Mark Ralston/AFP/Getty Images, (center) Barry Bland/ Barcroft Media/Getty Images, 86 s_bukley/Shutterstock.com, 87 (left) Con/Demotix/Corbis, (right) Barcroft Media via Getty Images, 88 Robertus Pudyanto/Getty Images, 89 (top) PA Images, (bottom) Stacie McChesney/NBC/NBCU Photo Bank via Getty Images, 90 (center) Shutterstock.com, (bottom) Yamil Lage/AFP/Getty Images, 90–91 Francisco Leong/AFP/Getty Images, 92 Imaginechina/Corbis, 93 (top) Shutterstock.com, (bottom) Gonzales Photo/Demotix/Corbis, (bottom right) Shutterstock.com, 94–95 Liam Cleary/Demotix, 96 Ilya S. Savenok/Getty Images, 97 Petri Oeschger/Gallo Images/Getty Images, 98–99 Imaginechina/REX/Shutterstock, 100 (left) AF archive/Alamy, (right) Kena Betancur/AFP/Getty Images, 101 (top) Ellen DeGeneres, (bottom) Shutterstock.com, 102 Geoffrey Robinson/REX/Shutterstock, 103 (right) Laurence Griffiths/Getty Images, (center) NASA, 104 Andrew Savulich/NY Daily News Archive via Getty Images, 105 (top) Ruaridh Connellan/Barcroft USA via Getty Images, (bottom) Jack Ludlam/Alamy, 106 Shutterstock, 107 (top) Steve Russell/Toronto Star via Getty Images, (bottom) terstock, 108–109 Jim Watson/AFP/Getty Images, 110 FOX via Getty Images, 111 (top) Shutterstock (bottom), Ruaridh Connellan/Barcroft USA via Getty Images, 112 Shutterstock, 113 HAP/

Quirky China News/REX/Shutterstock, 114–115 Mark Campbell/REX/Shutterstock, 116 (top) Etihad Airways via Getty Images, (bottom) Rainer W. Schlegelmilch/Getty Images, 117 (top) Enrique De La Osa/Reuters, (center) Catherine Steenkeste/Getty Images, 118 Shutterstock.com, 119 (top) ParagonSpaceDevelopment/Splash/Splash News, (center) VCG/VCG via Getty Images, 120 (top) Eric Sakowski, (bottom) The Bund, 121 (top) Imaginechina/REX/Shutterstock, (center) © Raymond Cunningham, (bottom) Shutterstock, 122 Shutterstock, 123 (top) Ministry of Fisheries via Getty Images, (bottom) RSPCA, 124 NASA, 125 (top) Clement Mahoudeau/IP/Getty Images, (bottom) Zhejiang University, 126 (left) Geraldo Caso/AFP/Getty Images, (right) Aflo/REX/Shutterstock, 127 Austral Int./REX/Shutterstock, 128 (top) Johan Ordonez/AFP/Getty Images, (bottom) Vent Haven Museum, 129 Shutterstock, 130–131 Adnan Abidi/Reuters, 132 Shutterstock.com, 133 (top) Pau Barrena/AFP/Getty Images, (bottom) Jeff Spicer/Getty Images for Leapfrog Films, 35 Yoshikazu Tsuno/AFP/Getty Images, 136 & 137 (top) Shutterstock, (bottom) Justin Tallis/AFP/Getty Images, 138 (top) Nokian Tyres, (bottom) Jeff Gross/Getty Images, 139 Tim Defrisco/Getty Images, 140–141 Garth Milan/Red Bull Photofiles via Getty Images, 142 Caters News Agency, 143 (top) Shutterstock, (bottom) Katie Greene/Bellingham Herald/MCT via Getty Images, 144 (top) Omar Torres/AFP/Getty (bottom) Shutterstock, 145 Topical Press Agency/Hulton Archive/Getty Images, 146 Marcos Mesa Sam Wordley/Shutterstock, 147 REX/Shutterstock, 148–149 Justin Tallis/AFP/Getty Images, 150 Toru Yamanaka/AFP/Getty Images, 151 Shutterstock, 152 (center) Imaginechina/REX/Shutterstock, (bottom) AFP Photo/Peter Parks/Getty Images, 153 (top) Big Swing, (bottom) Harry How/Getty Images, 154 (top) KeystoneUSA-ZUMA/REX, (bottom) Steve Shott/Getty Images, 155 (left) Adrees Latif/Reuters, (right) Arkaprava Ghosh/Barcroft India, 160 HAP/Quirky China News/REX/Shutterstock

Every effort has been made to acknowledge correctly and contact the source and/or copyright holder of each photograph and Carlton Books Limited apologizes for any unintentional errors or omissions, which will be corrected in future editions of this book.